Mary Perkins Ives Abbott

The Beverleys

A Story of Calcutta

Mary Perkins Ives Abbott

The Beverleys
A Story of Calcutta

ISBN/EAN: 9783744705011

Printed in Europe, USA, Canada, Australia, Japan

Cover: Foto ©Thomas Meinert / pixelio.de

More available books at **www.hansebooks.com**

THE BEVERLEYS

A Story of Calcutta

BY

MARY ABBOTT

AUTHOR OF "ALEXIA"

CHICAGO

A. C. McCLURG AND COMPANY

1890

THE BEVERLEYS.

CHAPTER I.

THE Winterfords were at breakfast, and Eileen had not yet come down. It was late; but it always is late in India, — that is to say, in the households of men in any of the services, civil, military, and forensic. The head of this one — if it could be said to have a head, or if Barney Winterford could be said to be the head of anything — had nothing more exigent on most days than the exercising of his saddle-horses to demand his early morning attention. He had not even been out for his usual gallop this time, but was sleepily assimilating a scolding, with his curry and rice, from his wife, Philippa.

Philippa — in other words, Lady Barney Winterford — had rarely allowed herself to descend to the rôle of a fault-finder until lately, although she might have done so at any moment for seventeen years, with every excuse in life. Remonstrance, vain but irresistible, was becoming more of a habit with her latterly, however; for she found her patience pretty well at an end. A long course of separation from her children, of jungle-fevers, and all kinds of malarial distempers, — for they had not always been lodged sumptuously in Calcutta, — and a very long and trying course of her husband, Barney, had worn a temper once of the sweetest to a point, and that a sharp one.

Philippa had been out in India a good many years. Seven children had been born to her, from each of whom, one after the other, she had been obliged to sever herself with a mighty wrench. Until this last year there had always been one child young enough to stay with her; but Biddy, the baby, was five, and Philippa, in a real agony, had left the last precious one with its grandfather in England, knowing it dangerous to the child's health to keep it any longer in a hot climate. It was a terrible blow to her; no one, from her haughty and self-contained demeanor, suspected how terrible. And although she had never up to this time swerved from her fidelity to Barney, — who, to say truth, was not exactly the man to be cast loose on his own recognizances in a gay country like India, — Philippa was fast losing her steadfastness, and her self-control too, and showed her utter weariness of spirit by ordinary apathy to most persons and things, and now and then extraordinary severity to Barney.

It was his sixteenth year in India, this bad Barney, and he was only now magistrate of the " 24-Pergunnahs " in Calcutta. Men who had never blinked at an eastern sun until long after Barney had been dried and seasoned by a many years' process of them, were drawing handsome salaries as High Court Judges or officers of the Viceroy's Council. It had been Barney's own fault, — his bad luck, of course he said. He had done wild things in his youth, and middle age had not steadied him to slowness. He was, not to put too fine a point upon it, good for nothing ; and Philippa knew it.

Besides all this as one may say chronic grievance, the subject of the breakfast-table philippic was another and an acuter cause of complaint.

Anything sweeter or more peaceful than the scene it would be hard to find. As Philippa sat in her high-backed wrought-ebony chair, she could gaze, through wide French window-ways, with arches of shrubbery for further frames, at lovely flowering trees, and ivies, and all kinds of tropic wonders, growing in gay profusion. The air was blossoming with fairy orchids ; pointzettias and bright red hibiscus made flames of color in the glowing distance. In the foreground were the aloes and the yucca and the commoner garden flowers, — the brighter ones having taken to themselves Oriental dyes, it seemed ; for a color must be vivid in India or the sun fades every vestige of hue from it. The air was filled with sweetness, not pungent, but languid. The very roses, which are gay and self-asserting in a colder clime, are delicate and faint, like women under the same conditions, in an eastern air. The room in which Philippa sat — as discontented a woman as ever sat — was full of softness and luxury and perfume. Crystal lamps hung from the ceiling by broad bands of crimson silk ; the curtains were of the same rich hue and of a marvellous texture ; rugs of the deepest, softest pile covered the tessellated floor, — for this was the cold weather, although its rigors were hardly extreme.   Turbaned and draped retainers awaited in silence the faintest breath of behest.   Everything spoke of comfort and of ease.   How little was of either in that barren house !

" You know very well, Barney," Philippa was saying, as she toyed with her fruit, " I have sacrificed myself in everything.   I was willing enough to bring Eileen out the first time, and to do all in my power to marry her well and to keep her from throwing herself away on that wretch.   And in spite of her idiotic refusals of fine offers, and her suicidal acceptance of the worst one she had ; in spite of her escapades and follies, in every one of which you encouraged her, Barney," — a twinkle came into Barney's eye, — " you know how fond I have always been of Eileen, even although you have spent more on her than you have ever spent on your own children." Barney sighed resignedly.   " When it came to bringing her out the second time, — a young widow, with no signs of widowhood about her except her independence, and with all those shocking clouds hanging over her, — it was too much for me to undertake, I felt ; and yet I tried to do my best then.   But now that she is going on in exactly the same old way, flirting wildly with ineligible men, spending no end of money, and giving one more than one can possibly do to look after her, without the excuses of youth and inexperience she had before, I say, Barney, that something must be done to stop it.   And if you

won't take some step, I must.   I am not called upon
to endure this sort of thing any longer, and Eileen
is ruining herself."   Philippa had never in her life
spoken so explicitly to Barney; but her speech had
gathered impetus as it rose from her lips.

Ordinarily, Barney Winterford was one mass of
good-nature.   Your harum-scarums mostly are.   He
could not argue, for several reasons; one being his
ignorance of any coherent line, and another his lazi-
ness, — it was too much trouble.   But Eileen was his
idol, — his sister, and the one person who combined,
for him, all human attraction.   He never heard her
disparaged without a protest.   "My darlin'," he said,
sleepy still, but not without a flush, "when will you
learn not to exaggerate?   You mean Jack Beverley,
I suppose, when you say 'ineligible' men and
Eileen is 'flirting wildly,' because he is no good as
a *parti*, and because she won't look at old Warwick,
who's a catch.   I wish she would marry Warwick;
you know how I've tried to bring it about.   But
she won't.   If Jack were a match now, you would
say Eileen was behaving most discreetly in encouraging him.   I don't know that she is leading him
on any more than a dozen others.   How the men
do like her!"

"Like her?   Of course they like her.   No one
can help liking her.   But only the poverty-stricken
younger sons — and Mr. Warwick — want to marry
her.   Men like anybody who is pretty and fascinating, and amuses them, and has a good seat on a
horse.   But Eileen can't afford to go in for that sort
of thing alone.   She must look for something else;

and she's not a girl any more, to be wasting her
time and her looks, as she does."

"Well, what is she then?" retorted Barney.
"Faith, she's not one-and-twenty, and had misery
enough with that brute Beaufort to last a score of
years. As for giving you more than you can manage to look after her, my love, when was that? We
sent you home from the Friths' ball at one; and
did n't I look after the child myself, — and I blind
in both eyes from sleep?" ·

"Yes, there's an instance," quickly broke in Philippa, — "that ball! Eileen was fairly stared at the
whole night. So free and off-hand in her manner, —
so gay, and as if she had not a care! Valsing madly
about like a top, and going on for all the world like
an American! Her looks, bearing, those of a girl
of eighteen, at most!"

"And just as long as she can look eighteen, I
hope she will then," replied Barney, whose sleepi-
ness had entirely departed. "If she keeps her
smooth skin and her merry laugh and her yellow
hair, like a baby's, I'll be the last man to begrudge
them to her, the lamb!" Barney had not shown
much anxiety to preserve Philippa's skin or her hair
or her laugh, but I doubt if he would have done
much more than talk about Eileen's. "If she
were to have nothing but wild merriment from now
till the day of her death, and that fifty years hence,
it would not make up for the agony that girl has
suffered. It's precious few, now I tell you, Philippa,
who go through half Eileen has done, or bear it
with half her spirit."

"I know all about her sufferings, Barney, as well as you," said Philippa; "and if it were a question of mad merriment only, she might make the welkin ring with it, and I should be charmed, I'm sure. But there's very little merriment ahead for her," she said, changing her tone, and speaking gravely, "unless she will honestly try to help herself. Why can't she marry Mr. Warwick? He is not old, although you call him so (and I wish you wouldn't before her, Barney), — he is not a *parvenu;* he is very gentlemanlike — and fabulously rich."

"I don't know why she won't," said Barney, in a low tone.

Philippa went on: "Eileen has never been taunted, as she might have been with reason sometimes, as the cause of all her own misfortunes. If she had not run counter to all our wishes, and thrown herself away upon a horrid wretch, she would never have been in this ridiculous position. Then she would pay off a lot of Aleck Beaufort's gambling debts; and the result is, our innocent pockets — innocent of money as well as of Eileen's obligations — suffer, for she can't dress even on her own income. If you were not so free with your money, Barney, showering it on these men, who seem to me to live at your expense, one might not have to be so perpetually fretted. But to see our small means squandered, our children never destined to anything more than a writing acquaintance with their parents, — for I don't see but that we shall have to stay here forever, — our lives going, my health shattered!"

It was not like this most self-contained of women
to go on thus, and Barney thought he heard a faint
sob.   This would have brought him to his knees, if
his wife had not resumed, having stopped to take
breath merely.

" Ida has written me only lately that it seems to
her grossly unfair that Gerald should have to sup-
port their children, when you do not one thing for
ours."   Ida was Philippa's sister, and Gerald her
husband.   " Their Alan is old enough to go to a
public school, and they have to pinch to send him ;
and here is our Barney, she says, sailing off to
Rugby without a penny from you.   It is an old
story, Barney, — I know you are tired of hearing
about it, as indeed am I of talking, — but a change
must come.   Papa sees the justice of Ida's feeling,
as indeed must we, Barney.   He writes so gently,
and yet I know he is embarrassed.   It is terribly
trying to me."

And this time Barney was sure he heard a sob.
It was an unwonted sound from that quarter.   He
might be coming to the end of his tether.   He
must pacify her.   " Don't cry, Flip," he said gently
across the table ; " don't worry, darlin' !   I sold
Polly for fourteen hundred rupees yesterday, and
the Governor has just sent me a hundred pounds.
I 'll soon have Dankipore," — this was a magistracy
for which Barney had longed, not enough to make
an effort for it, however, for years, — " and you shall
have Biddy on your knee in another six months, if
you choose to go home."

While Barney was uttering the first words, he

was regretting them. He had not intended to tell
Philippa of the money, nor indeed had he meant to
put it to any useful purpose whatever. And to tell
the truth, he had partly promised to lend a good
deal of it to an impecunious brother dare-devil with
less means than himself, and no conscience at all.
Well, he was in for it now.

Philippa brightened. It gave her a thrill to know
that they really had an extra penny; but she knew
that unless she could get it into her own hands,
they might as well not have had it. She smiled
upon her husband. "What could have come
in more handily?" she said brightly. "Were you
going to surprise me with it? Send papa the hundred pounds; it will relieve him and me, and it
will start Barney at school, at all events. Why, it
will almost keep him there a twelvemonth. You 'll
do it, won't you, dear?" she asked anxiously, for
Barney's face had fallen. It no longer seemed odd
and unnatural for a mother to be pleading to a father
for his own children. Years had made a usage of
it. The first thing now was to make Barney promise,
and the next, to see that he kept his word ; for Barney
had been known to wriggle out of very minute aper-
tures ; and slips betwixt cups and lips were familiar
commodities to the Lady Barney Winterford.

Barney had risen from his place, and was standing
now near the door. Philippa too rose, and ap-
proaching him, looked appealingly into Barney's
face. "Yes, yes, my love, I 'll send it, I 'll send it,"
he said with impatience. " I 'm sorry your father
has to pay my son's schooling. You see you ought

never to have married a beggar." And Barney
drew himself up to his full height, as if he had said
prince instead. He could be very dignified on
ready money, even although it was a short-lived
glory. "I'm grieved Ida should have had to write
you such a nasty, jealous letter." And Barney fan·
cied himself wounded and indignant. If he was, it
was at having to pay the money.

But that promise — he had not made it before
he had resolved to break it. Only, this *tête-à-tête*
must end. Barney did not care to repeat words
which might rise inconveniently to confront him;
and Philippa might ask him to swear. She had
done that before.

Barney jarred his bearer, who was about to present a small silver stand upon which glowed a ball
of fire, — for Barney was twiddling in his fingers
an unlighted cheroot. The ball fell to the floor,
and was dashed into a hundred fiery fragments
on the rug. "Son of a pig!" remarked Barney,
calmly, in Hindustani, hardly glancing at the unfortunate Hindu, who was dancing wildly upon the
glowing coals to put them out. Philippa did not
even turn; it was too every day an occurrence;
the goolies were forever dropping about, and the
servants never burned their feet. They would not
presume.

Barney lighted his cheroot at one of the still
burning bits, which the bearer had hastily placed
with his fingers back upon the stand. Then he
sauntered through the hall to the big middle doorway. He thought he heard a horse's step upon the

drive. What a fool he had been to tell Philippa about that money! "Barney," she said hastily, "here comes somebody. Promise me that you will say nothing about the fourteen hundred rupees until I can talk with you further; and send the hundred pounds to England to-day." But there was no time to answer; the man had dismounted, and was running up the porte-cochère steps.

The new-comer was named Stanhope, captain by courtesy, — in reality a lieutenant, and an aide-de-camp to the Viceroy, — a short, thick-set fellow, rather handsome, not very bad, but the very man Philippa hated most in Calcutta. For he seemed to possess the faculty — all men had it, or could have had it, for the cultivation, but this one possessed it in a supreme degree — of getting money out of her husband; and Philippa knew that Captain Stanhope could smell fourteen hundred rupees in the air, and come swooping down upon them like an adjutant or a buzzard. So Philippa held out a gracious hand, and smiled sweetly. He was to be conciliated above all things, and fascinated if possible, and kept away from Barney.

Most women are faded in India; and Philippa still passed for a beauty, when no fresher ones were by. She had a statuesque, high-bred face, and had been a beauty in her day. Her hair was still good, and her eyes fine. As for her figure, it was perfect; and men said she alone in India knew how to walk.

"Your garden is so much better than mine, Lady Barney," said Stanhope, "that I like to come in and look at it. How well your hibiscus grows!

That double yellow bush near the gate is the finest thing I ever saw."

"Yes," said Barney, with a mocking look at Stanhope, "thousands come to see that bush every day! Beautiful thing, is n't it? Hibiscus is so uncommon in India too. There are n't more than a dozen bushes in every compound!"

"Don't mind him, Mr. Stanhope," said Philippa, playfully, making up her mind she would not allow this man to leave her, unless to walk into Eileen's hands. He should not have a private talk with Barney, until that money was disposed of. "Will you come up to the veranda," she said, "or shall we go to the stables and see Eileen's new Arab? I want to ask you what you think of her mounting such a wild animal." They walked in the direction of the stables, a chuprassi running after them with a scarlet umbrella, which he held over the lady's head; and Stanhope had hardly time for a word, Philippa was so voluble and gracious. It was so overdone, her manner, that neither Barney nor Stanhope was deceived by it.

Barney still stood in the doorway smoking. He could yet afford to be in tolerable spirits; although he had made promises to both his wife and Stanhope, he might be able to escape both. Stanhope would not be easy to shake off; but Philippa — pooh! He blew a cloud of smoke and smiled serenely. "Why, *why*," he said, after a moment to himself, "must I be such an egregious idiot as to tell everything I know? I 'm like a baby. The fact is, I am so deucedly soft-hearted and confiding that

I injure myself all the time. I might have known Flip would make me do some confounded useful thing or other with that money. I'm hanged if I'll pay a bill. Where's the pleasure that lucre is supposed to give a man, if he has to pay it right away for worn-out coats, and dinners that were not only eaten long ago, but which very likely disagreed with him? No, I'll not — "

As Lord Barney Winterford stood in the great doorway, framed in thick verdure, his hands in the pockets of his white flannel coat, his honest eyes and his cravat as blue as the skies, his blond hair parted carefully down the middle, and a general air of candor and fresh young innocence about him, you would have staked your life upon his perfect truth ; and, gentle or ungentle reader, I need not tell you whether you would have lost your valuable stake or not.

Barney was interrupted by another visitor, an adorer of his sister's this time, the very Jack Beverley whom Philippa had called ineligible. He was a great favorite of Barney's, perhaps for the reason that he was his exact antipodes. "Arrah, then," called out the host, "keep off the grass ! What are you doing in a gentleman's compound ? " and he sprang down the steps, seized the Captain by the waist, and threw him. The other was more than a match for Barney, however ; and as, after a few moments of wrestling, Captain Beverley stood over his fallen foe, his hand outstretched in a theatrical attitude, he looked up suddenly and flushed with something more than victory, for there was a vision in the doorway.

2

CHAPTER II.

A PRETTY, a very pretty creature was Eileen Beaufort. Tall and straight she was, and slight; with Irish eyes, — those great, heavily veiled, dark gray eyes, with no end to the possibilities in their depth nor the depths in their possibilities; with gold wavy hair, — deep gold, not the usual blond, — shading her white forehead; with lips that were dewy and bright, and with a skin of cream and roses, — rare indeed in India. A mocking, sweet-lipped goddess Eileen looked, as she stood, framed by lycopodium and panax, in the wide doorway. Her eyes were fixed upon the two men, one of whom looked a trifle embarrassed, as he came laughing up the steps.

"Oh, Barney, you baby!" cried the goddess, rippling into laughter, with a touch of scorn, as Barney rose from the grass, displaying large green spots upon his white raiment. "To wrestle in this heat too! You are just as foolish, Captain Beverley, only I dare not say so! Is not that truly Irish?" she added archly, holding out a hand to the younger man. "I have not breakfasted yet; you may both come and see me eat an egg and an ortolan, if you like."

"Ortolans for breakfast !" shouted Barney. "You 'll ruin me with your extravagance. Besides, there are n't any (Irish again) ; so don't deceive yourself."

"I only said it on account of the two vowels sounding well together, literal person !" said Eileen. "Don't disturb yourself, embodiment of frugality ! I have ordered nothing costly."

Barney patted his sister on the back. If he had a strength, — one could hardly call it a weakness in such a character, — it was his fondness for Eileen.

Captain Beverley followed into the breakfast-room with joy undisguised in every movement. His admiration for Eileen was unfeigned and unconcealed.

Barney strode through the huge room, and stood on the back veranda, whistling softly to the birds in their cages there. He usually devoted a few minutes each day to the birds, and a good many minutes to the horses and dogs of his establishment. He rode hard, but never abused an animal ; and all the beasts adored him. The aviary included a large cage of quail which had been bought to fatten for the table. "I should as soon think of eating my own children as those things I 've been feeding and petting !" Barney exclaimed, when there was a talk of despatching them. So the collection grew, owing to Barney's soft-heartedness. And he who willingly saw his own offspring fed and petted by his wife's relations, and who knew little or nothing of his children's joys and sorrows, would shed tears at the sight of one of his pets in pain. Barney's tears were near the surface, and the water was shallow.

Another step was heard, — on the gravel walk at

the garden side of the house this time, — and Barney
looked out.   Jack's father, Colonel Beverley, — a
magnificent, soldierly man, not sturdier than Jack, but
far more showy,— had appeared upon the scene.   He
might almost have been Jack's brother, if you did
not scan his face too closely and discover the lines
there.   Jack was like his father in certain turns of
the head and motions of the shoulders and arms ;
and his face took on now and then, but rarely, that
sudden resemblance which disappears like a flash-
light before you can recognize it or give it a name.
Jack was called a plain presentment of his father.
The Colonel was certainly handsomer ; his telling
eyes were in constant use and knew many wonderful
tricks ; these, together with his superb gray mustache, his impressed manner, and his great air of
distinction, had been fatal to the peace of mind of
many a woman, whereas Jack had hardly had a conquest.   Jack was younger naturally, and then he had
not learned as yet many arts.   His mustache was a
trifle ragged, and his eyes were not trained to execu-
tion.   And then he was run in another mould.

Barney made a salaam to the new-comer, and
moved forward to meet him.   The Colonel replied
to the salute by a cut across his host's legs with his
walking-stick.   It was evident that Barney and his
friends were on informal terms.

"How are you, Paddy?" said the visitor.
"Did n't I see Jack disappear into the house by the
other doorway?   I thought I could cut him off at
this end.   What is he doing here?   Boring Lady
Barney and your sister, I 'll be bound.   By the by,

Barney, what a glorious picture Lady Ellen made last night at the Friths'! She's the handsomest being Calcutta has seen for many a long day."

"Bad blood!" said Barney, shrugging his shoulders and motioning over them, to show that he might be overheard. The two sauntered down the gravel walk. "Philippa has been giving me Cain about her this morning." Barney always told everything he knew to anybody. "There's no accounting for women, Bev, except that you may be sure the pretty ones will have to catch it!"

"And the ugly ones too," said the Colonel, dryly. "I'd rather catch what the pretty ones get and take the risks. But what has Lady Ellen done now? Has she been flirting too palpably with my poor child? He's taken to poetry, Barney," said the Colonel, stopping short and bursting into a laugh; "and when a fellow without a brain in his head takes to that, he's pretty bad. The boy is getting beyond me though, truly. Here he is, an ugly dog, without a farthing in his pocket, — in debt, I believe, — and he's already been going on so with that girl the Olmsteads brought out, — what's her name? Sidney Markham, — that I'm positively ashamed to meet any of the family. Now, here he is, boring Lady Ellen into her grave. He's really in earnest this time, no doubt, or thinks he is. But the fool can't marry, even if Lady Ellen consented to think of such a cub. I wish you'd stop the thing, Barney, if you have any influence; 'pon my honor, I do. I'm helpless, you know."

Barney, who liked Jack, felt the blood mounting

to his temples. He hardly knew why he was angry either. The Colonel had implied nothing derogatory to Eileen exactly, and yet — Barney was never quite clear in his reasoning — he had, a great deal. Jack had been at Eileen's feet ever since he had met her, — not many weeks, to be sure. He had ridden with her or after her every day; had walked with her in the Eden gardens, and in their own garden in the early mornings, when she was up. He had been fishing for invitations to dinner, Barney thought indignantly, so as to be near her; he had come calling at all hours, had even dared to start and blush whenever Eileen's name was mentioned, or she looked at him. Jack was too honest, Barney had always thought, to dissemble. But whether he was honest or not, Eileen could not afford to marry him. He resolved to keep his eyes open now. If his sister had been played with — and by an unprincipled beggar, by Jove ! The blood of all the Winterfords boiled within him, and his manly brow mantled.

There was no time to reply, for his wife and Stanhope now appeared from the stables, and Barney, who had forgotten the green grass-stains, was now reminded of them by Philippa, and went into the house to interview his bearer on the subject of a fresh coat. "Your papa's out there, looking for you," he said satirically to Jack, as he passed through the room again. Jack showed no signs of stirring, only smiled; but at a word from Eileen, he went out.

There were four in the party now; for Captain Carbury, another aide at Government House, had

joined the three. The air was delicious, out of the
sun ; but in the sun it was always hot. They were
standing, when Jack went out, under a huge banyan-
tree, near the gate. The banyan was old, and had
thrown half a hundred shoots into the ground at
various points in its career, each shoot being now
firmly rooted ; and some of them were as thick as
the trunk of a young maple. At some epoch the
banyan must have offered his hand and heart to a
young peepul-tree ; for the peepul had joined her
lot to the banyan's, and both were firmly rooted together now in a common stem. They were not perfectly of one mind, however, in minor matters ; for
the banyan shed his leaves at one season and the
peepul hers at another, and when the former was
rejoicing in dark glossy leaves and red berries, the
latter had just put forth her tender, light green
shoots. The venerable couple shaded the lawn for
some distance, and under the branches our party sat
down, servants having first spread a blue and white
durree.

The Winterfords' garden was the resort at this
time of day or earlier, usually, for this set of men.
Philippa usually appeared, and Eileen ; and sometimes they had tennis, after their morning rides.
But in the coldest weather — this was it ! — they
did not always ride early, nor even rise, and after
a ball they were much later. This was a holiday
too.

" What early hours we all keep ! " the Colonel was
saying, when Jack joined the party. " Jack, you
hound, what were you doing in a lady's breakfast-

room? Go to work and earn something to keep your poor old father in idleness."

"Work on a holiday! Unnatural father!" said Jack, laughing. "To tell the truth, I did do some work this morning. I finished my day's labor before you had stirred, Dad," he added, looking at his father with beaming eyes. "You may now lounge with your hands in your pockets the rest of the day. I have provided for you."

"Faith, there may be a good bit of truth in that same," muttered Barney, who had just come out, to Stanhope. He had not quite forgiven the Colonel his taunt.

Philippa, poor soul, was devising a scheme by which she could keep her husband and Captain Stanhope apart. They were sitting a few steps from the rest when Eileen came out, with a train of dogs fawning upon her. Her filmy white dress draped itself gracefully about her figure; her hair gleamed in the sun. Every man sprang to his feet; a servant glided to her with an umbrella. "Well, well, what a levee!" she said in her bright young voice and with her bright young smile, "and I out of it! I am sure you are going in for politics or plots or some dreadful thing. Can't I know? No, on second thought, don't tell me. I should be sure to tell. I can't keep anything. Perhaps I had better withdraw?" And Eileen looked up archly at the Colonel, who was gazing broadly at her.

"Don't!" he answered solemnly. "There'll be 'plots' to murder one another, if you do. If you tell our secrets, Lady Ellen, you'll convict yourself.

I came to find Jack, the lost heir. When he is mis-
laid, I usually look for him here. He came to look
for me, no doubt!" Jack laughed, and flickered
a few leaves off the banyan-tree with his walking-
stick gayly. "Stanhope and Carbury can find their
own excuses."

"No excuse is needed, except for staying away,"
said Captain Carbury. "A certificate of lunacy
would be required for a man who had the *entrée*
here, if he did not make use of it. I came to see
the ladies, and I'm the only one who dares own
it, it seems."

"Your house is the loveliest in Calcutta, and the
jolliest, Lady Barney," said Stanhope, throwing himself at Philippa's feet, and ignoring the last speaker.
"I told the Viceroy so only yesterday."

"And did n't he say he knew it?" laughed
Eileen. "I trust our efforts were not thrown away
upon him on the last awful occasion of his dining
here. We had about twenty extra khidmutgars in,"
she said, looking at the Colonel, "and an additional
cook; consequently no decent food. We spent the
entire day in worrying and changing things about;
and all for a man one would entertain quite simply
in England. I don't know why we do it. The house
was a great deal nicer as it was; and nothing is so
silly as unwonted splendor."

"There was no splendor about it," Philippa said,
a little impatiently; "but of course, when one enter-
tains the Viceroy, one must have more — more — "

"There! you can't find a name for it, and that's
why I hate it," cried Eileen, — "that more some-

thing that you have to have. My sovereign, or my sovereign's representative, shall dine with me as I am in the future, or not at all." ("He would prefer you as you are, I'm sure," murmured Colonel Beverley, fervently.) "Not one change will I ever make again."

"What change did you make, pray?" laughed Philippa, not without a tinge of tartness. "I observed nothing specially conventional about you."

"Oh, but there was!" answered Eileen. "You should have seen me!" turning to Jack and Carbury, who were at her left. "I was almost regal in my bearing, and I wore my very best frock. An unknown khidmutgar spilled *petits pois* down my back too, and ruined the frock in a scuffle, and Barney's fish came in after the entrées. I saw it. Our own simple ways are good enough for any viceroy, and I shall tell him so the next time I see him."

"Lord love you!" exclaimed Colonel Beverley, "you don't call an Indian establishment simple, when an unpretending bachelor has to have twenty servants in order to exist! I call the simplest household in Calcutta a mass of pure extravagance and waste!"

"You're the last one to live without all that 'extravagance and waste,'" said Jack, laughing. His tone was invariably affectionate to his father. "I often wonder, though, when I see these black fellows lying about, doing nothing most of the time, — not worth the dhal or ghee or whatever it is they feed on, — that we submit to such imposition. It's little

enough each one costs ; but when it comes to forty
or fifty, it counts up enormously. Why does n't
somebody take a stand and change things about
a bit? "

" Oh, because," Philippa replied, " you could n't
teach them in a hundred years to do any more than
they have always done, or to do what they do differently. You try dismissing what seems to you an utterly ridiculously superfluous servant, — one whom
you have never seen do a single service, — and your
household arrangements go to pieces. The next
time one wants one's punkah pulled or some little
thing fetched, they are a man short, and nobody is on
hand to do it. I know ; I 've tried so many times to
cut down our staff. Perfect misery was the result."

" Oh, yes," said Barney, languidly, " what 's the
use? You 've got to submit, and you may as well
do it gracefully as fret yourself into heat apoplexy.
When the fellow who buttons your shoes won't
butter your toast, let them arrange it between them.
For my part, I have done my best to abolish the
caste-system. I try hard to mix my Hindus and
Mohammedans up, but it 's no go. They refuse to
sit on the same rug, even. Do you remember the
conflict you had with my bearer one day, Flip? "

" I do," said Philippa ; " I shall never forget it."

"What was it? " asked Eileen. " I never heard
of it."

" Oh, it was just an ordinary occurrence," Philippa
answered, " or might be. I never happened to
meet with that peculiar complication before. My
ayah, who is a Mehtranee, you know, was sitting in

the carriage, with her back to the horses, holding
Biddy, and we were just starting out for a drive. It
looked a little like a shower, and I sent Barney's
bearer up for a cloak for Biddy.   He gave it a toss
into the carriage in a most disrespectful way.   I told
him to hand it me properly.   He salaamed, gave
me an imploring glance, and told the syce to
take the cloak out of the carriage.   The syce's
hands were just off the horses' bridles, and I did
not wish him to touch a white cloak.   Besides, it was
too disobedient ; so I said to the bearer, ' Lift the
cloak from the floor yourself,' — it had fallen down,
— ' and hand it me.'   No.   The ayah then began to
weep, and Biddy joined in the outcry.   I was firm
with the bearer, who kept on salaaming, and at last
prostrated himself nearly under the wheels.   The
ayah thereupon got out, and the bearer hopped up,
and handed the cloak in.   The ayah's clothes had been
touching mine, it seemed, and so the bearer would
have defiled himself, if he had given me anything,
while she was in such close contact.   It was a
longer scene than I have made it even.   I believe I
dismissed the bearer, who said calmly he would
rather give up his place than lose his caste."

"Poor little ayah ! " cried Eileen.   "Worth a
dozen of him too !   How humiliated they must
feel, those low-caste creatures ! "

"Quite the contrary," said Philippa.   "It was
the bearer who looked ashamed ; the ayah begged
me not to insist, and was triumphant, as she flew
out, with her little bare brown feet.   This caste-
business does not prevent their being the best of

friends either. I heard the two discussing the affair
with great good-nature, later."

" We had a pathetic scene here one morning,"
Eileen said. " One of our bearers — yours again,
was n't it, Barney?— appeared suddenly before us, his
clothes dishevelled, his paint smudgy, his face distorted. Of course he wanted money. A hen had
walked in at the door of his hut, and had eaten out
of one of his lootahs or sorais, spread on the floor,
with his dinner in them. Every utensil had to be
thrown away, and we were to give him money for a
new set, of course."

" That 's a very old dodge," said Lady Barney,
" my father's servants did that. And yet, in spite
of all these tricks and bothers of Barney's bearer,
there is not a better servant in all India. He can
be trusted with anything; he is temperate, clean,
patient, and hard-working, for a native."

The bearer's ears must have burned, if he understood English; for he was among the party
all this time, handing lights, bringing footstools,
looking after everybody's needs. His face betrayed
nothing — not a ray of intelligence, even — at compliment or its reverse. Even an English servant, of
the highest possible perfection, could hardly have
preserved a more stoical composure. And yet, if
Barney had spoken seriously of dismissing him,
Kali Dass would have come to his master at his first
opportunity, and implored patience and another
trial. Who can fathom the ways of these dusky
retainers?

" All that nonsense about caste is tiresome and

stupid," said Stanhope; "and yet, if caste were
abolished we should not have the service we have
now. I took a Christian bearer once, to please
my mother, who goes in for missionary very strong
["What a field opened before her in her own family!" thought Philippa]; and the result was—
wretchedness. That man with caste had laid off
cleanliness and abstemiousness, drank my wine,
smoked my cheroots, wore creaking boots, answered
me disrespectfully in horrible English, — did everything that was excruciating, in short, — and I was
only too happy to exchange him for one of the old
sort. Orthodox Hindus make the only bearable
bearers."

"I don't know why you call the creature you
described a Christian," said Eileen, rather warmly.
"He was simply de-Hinduized, and had nothing
in the place of his old creed."

"It's astonishing," broke in Philippa, who could
not endure a religious discussion, and who thought
she saw one coming, "how little we put up with
from servants here. One fault, and off they go."

"That is the law of supply and demand," said
Carbury. "Perfection is a commodity; and if one
can get it for the same price one pays for stupidity,
of course stupidity goes."

"I wish," sighed Eileen in a low tone, as if she
were ashamed of it, "that we felt our responsibilities more in regard to these races. But people
yawn in one's face if one even mentions these
great daily problems. I must confess they worry
me." Eileen was blushing a little; she seldom

spoke seriously, and nobody in this party had ever heard her do so before.

"Your concern about the Hindus reminds me of Philippa's alarms about fires and burglars, when we are at home," laughed Barney. "Every three months or so, she has a terrible fright; wakes me up, and says, 'Barney, I cannot sleep a wink; I hear such strange noises, and I'm sure I smell smoke. Do get up and see!' Before I can stir, she is fast asleep again, and I never hear anything more about it until the next quarterly scare."

"Now, Barney," pouted Eileen, flippant again, "I am always devising schemes for the elevation of these people. I don't get much encouragement, it is safe to say, from *you!*"

"What have you done so far?" asked Philippa, a little satirically.

"Nothing at all," answered Eileen, wearily. "I have talked to my ayah; and her state, I find, is so much more hopeful than mine that I can't do anything for her. She goes to the Maidan *once a year*, and hears preaching in a foreign tongue, not a word of which does she understand. That is all the religious instruction she ever has; and yet, when I told her one day in the hot weather to start up the punkah-rope in my dressing-room, she folded both hands behind her, and looked at me supplicatingly. 'I cannot touch it, memsahib.' 'Who will know?' I said impatiently. (The very idea of that stupid punkah-wallah downstairs calling himself her superior, made me furious!) 'God will know,' she replied reverently. I felt abashed in the presence of such simple goodness. And then I need so many improvements myself that I feel rather modest about attempting to improve those who seem to need it less. A pagan who has had every advantage is without excuse."

"I deny that you are a pagan, or that you need improvement," broke in Colonel Beverley. (Jack could not for the world have made a pretty speech then; that was one difference between them.)

"Oh, I am, and I do," laughed Eileen, shaking off her seriousness again. "Not that I expect you to believe me; if I did, I should not say it."

"Eileen is right," said Philippa, gently, giving the girl a tenderer glance than she had done for months, "about the conscientiousness of some of the lowest castes. But the question of awakening them to new responsibilities is outside of all that. Of course it is our duty to show them the right way, and we don't do it. We don't lead the lives we should, to begin with."

"It would be a case of the blind who won't see leading the blind who can't, would n't it?" laughed Eileen. "We should have to begin at the beginning, and unlearn and forget first, then be taught all over again. Right is wrong, and wrong right to me, I am so perverted."

It was rather a singular group, — Colonel Beverley and Captains Stanhope and Carbury contented to sit quietly by and listen to a conversation, the subject of which ordinarily interested them so little. When Eileen spoke, every man listened. It had done much towards that perversion of which she had spoken.

" I have been out here only six months, to be sure,"
said Captain Stanhope ; " but this is the first time, I
give you my word of honor, I have ever heard native
servants mentioned, — that is to say, in society. I
wrote my mother last week that not a soul ever thought
of natives, or looked at them. I am glad to find that
somebody does occasionally bestow a thought on the
poor brutes."

" I 'm not glad, then," said Barney, stifling a yawn,
" if that somebody is in my family. Their religion
is good enough for them, and suits them to a turn ;
and I don't want to bother, for one, with reconstruct-
ing them. For pity's sake, let 's change the subject.
One would think this was a missionary meeting ! "

Eileen suddenly sprang to her feet. " Dear me,
Philippa," she said, " were n't we to go somewhere
this morning? I am such a slave to my engagement-
book I don't try to remember ; but were n't we to
ameliorate somebody's condition ? "

" And ' pessimate ' the condition of four men cor-
respondingly ? " said the Colonel. " How lovely and
lazy it is here ! The only drawback to enjoying the
beauties of Nature in England is that you feel so en-
ergetic ! Here there is a delicious lethargy which
completes one's idea of perfect enjoyment. May I
ride with you this evening ? " he asked suddenly, as
Eileen was giving him her hand.

Jack was disappointed ; he had looked forward to
a long interview with Eileen, which should be deci-
sive ; but his father's interest in her and admiration
for her pleased him, nevertheless. It was a tribute
to himself, he felt ; and after all, he was *sure* of her.

He managed, by following her up the steps, to say
one word. "There are ways," he said in a low tone,
"of doing something for our servants. I will help
you if I can. The missionaries know. Why should
we not go to them to find out how to begin?"

Eileen gave his hand a grateful clasp. "I may
not be in the mood long," she answered hurriedly.
"Don't think so well of me!"

"*Well* of her!" Jack's heart was bounding, as
he drove away. Think well of her! He was filled
to the brim with joy and bliss of her! The quick
glimpse she had given that morning of a desire to
live a higher life than the frivolous, butterfly existence they were all leading here, gave him a throb of
pleasure. He felt it so often himself; and stronger
than ever, as he drove over the Maidan, was his resolve
to give up his present occupation, — his flunkey work,
as he contemptuously called it, — and if his special
appointment was not forthcoming, to rejoin his regiment, and be at least a good soldier. "I must be
a man, not a monkey any more," he said to himself, —
"for her sake first and then for my own." And Jack,
who was as full of trust as of love, was flushed with
the happiness of eager anticipation. Would we could
all be content with our unrealized hopes! They are
the only happiness most of us ever know.

Poor Philippa, her worn face wreathed in tired
smiles, was still conversing with Stanhope. It was
a bootless task, however; she had no excuse for
staying out forever.

"Barney," she said at last, "will you come and
help me write that letter? I must get off an impor-

tant English document," she said, smiling, and extending a hand by way of farewell; "and Barney must do his share."

Barney looked at his watch. "By Jove!" he exclaimed. "It's after eleven, and I promised to meet Thorpe and Harcourt at half-past ten! When I come come back, Flip. There's plenty of time; the mail does n't close until night, you know." And the scamp called to his groom, who was sitting with his head on his knees beside Barney's trap. Barney hopped in, and took the reins. "Shall I drop you anywhere, Bev, Stanhope, Carbury, anybody?" he asked. No; they all had their own conveyances or horses waiting. But Captain Stanhope, who was riding, joined him outside the gate, and trotted beside him.

Philippa's morning's work had been hard and unavailing. (A gnat may sting an elephant, but it can hardly retard that animal's progress by standing in its way.

CHAPTER III.

EVERYBODY who knew Barney Winterford — and everybody did know him — knew that he had sold his fast horse, Polly, for fourteen hundred rupees. It was a public transaction, and Philippa must have been dreaming to suppose that the thing was a secret. Stanhope not only knew it as soon as Barney did himself, but it was through him that the sale was effected ! Barney, out of gratitude, had promised to lend the Captain part ; and a good deal more he had lost at cards the night before, at the Friths' ball. To tell the truth, Barney was a little uneasy ; he was decidedly in difficulties. Of course, it was only a question of time how soon he could squirm out, as he had done scores of times before ; but he was in for a pretty uncomfortable period until he did get out.

Barney, usually so reckless and easy-going, was a little sobered by his wife's serious air. She had seemed really determined, and he felt that when he went home to lunch — no, he would n't go home to lunch, that was too soon — but when he went home to dinner, she would have a draft of a letter to her father made out, stating that enclosed he would find one hundred pounds. Barney groaned.

Stanhope was at his side all this time. " Beverley wants us to lunch with him at the club," he said. " The new *chef*, you know, begins his *régime* to-day, and they say he 's a wonder."

Barney cheered up immediately. Not that he cared for his luncheon, — his own cook was a marvel too ; it was something to look forward to, something to do. The conclusion was foregone, and so was the money. Barney never could resist anybody or anything, but his duty.

He appeared at home just before his wife started for her drive before dinner; bankrupt again, but as easy and gay as ever.

Philippa had spent a very unhappy day. Pride would not allow her to write a complaining letter to her father; she had never done that yet, and she hoped, even knowing her husband so well, that he would keep his word given to her in the morning. But as soon as she saw him, her heart failed. He looked conscious, and his gayety was a trifle over-done.

" Have you done what you promised, Barney? " she asked anxiously, as they met on the upper landing.

Barney looked surprised. " Oh, you mean about sending the money to England? Flip, my love, I 'm awfully sorry, truly I am, but I can't do it. I was in debt out here, and you don't know how uncomfortable it made me." Philippa's lip curled. He had never been out of debt, except when her father had taken him out, since they had been married. " So I thought it better to pay off something here first."

Philippa turned a little giddy, but she steadied herself against the stair-rail. She had the letter in her desk, ready for the remittance. "Have you paid all we owe in Calcutta, Barney?" she asked, with a slight tremor of the lip, but looking him full in the face.

"Faith, no!" he laughed; "it would take more than I shall get in some time to do that. I have just quieted down a few of my creditors."

Philippa led the way into the drawing-room. Barney could not tell why he followed her, but he went like a lamb. Her desk was between two long windows, and the light shone full upon her white face, worn and set. Barney had never seen Philippa in quite this mood. He might have battled with hysterics or heroics; this style he could not understand. "Barney," she said, in a low, distinct tone, "I have a drawer filled with bills here; the tradesmen annoy me constantly about them. Will you give me a list of those you have paid? One hundred pounds is a thousand rupees, and fourteen hundred rupees more makes twenty-four hundred rupees. All the bills I have here amount to scarcely that. Have you paid these?"

Barney had been shifting from one foot to the other, and thrumming impatiently on the window-pane. He thrust aside the package of papers which Philippa held up, — gently, however. He made an attempt to laugh, and he took his wife's hand, which was cold. He really pitied her for the moment. She let him hold the hand, until he had answered her.

"My darlin'," said he, patting the hand, "you
know so little of business! These tradesmen's bills
are a small part of what I owe. The debts I have
paid are my own private ones, — debts of honor. I
have lost money at cards; I have had to lend
money; then personal loans have been made me;
I have borrowed, in short, from my friends."

"Will you oblige me with the names of those
friends?" asked Philippa, standing now, although
the room swam before her eyes.

"Why, how you go on, Flip!" he said contemptuously, by way of answer. "You are not like yourself. Why should you be bothered with these things?
I have often and often lost money, as you know;
often lent it, and oftener borrowed it. These are
my own private affairs. I can't tell you about them.
But I swear to you, Philippa —" His wife stopped
him with a violent gesture. She swept like a queen
to the stairway, down to her carriage, and into it.
Barney rushed out after her, and put her in. "If
you will wait a second for my hat, I'll drive with
you," he said.

"Chello! (Go on!)" to the coachman, was her
only reply.

That impressive Mohammedan, in his dark-
green Mahratta turban, made of twist after twist of
cloth, a twisted band of the green around his waist,
and his long white coat, cracked his whip; and the
grooms running ahead swiftly until the lodge-gate
was passed, then springing up behind, the carriage
was lost in a minute to Barney's view. He stood
on the step slightly dazed. "Dignity is her new

dodge, eh? She won't speak to me now for a week. I don't care. Stanhope is a good fellow, and will pay me when he can. I could n't see him in distress. How Philippa did glare at me! I wish I had gone with her. We should have had it out, at all events, and she could n't have said much on the course, with everybody looking on. Dear old Flip, how pretty she was, and what sweet coquettish ways she had! How women do age and change! This one won't," he added, as he heard his sister's step on the stair, and turned to look.

Eileen in her habit was Eileen at home. The grace which marked all her movements was consummated when she was dressed for her favorite exercise. "If Colonel Beverley is not on time," she said with a pout, "I shall not ride with him. I never waited a minute yet for a man. And there's nothing to detain one in Calcutta. Go and get ready, Barney, to ride with me, and be quick!"

But the clatter of hoofs was heard at that moment, and the lady was appeased. Barney saw them off, and his face was dark. He had lunched with the Colonel, entirely forgetting his momentary wrath of the morning. But as he saw them ride out together, he wished Eileen could make up her mind at once to marry Mr. Warwick and end all this nonsense. Things were getting horribly mixed up, he said to himself despondently, as he went to play tennis.

CHAPTER IV.

THERE is one fashionable drive in Calcutta, the Strand. It lies along the river-bank for two or three miles, a double line of beautiful stately ships almost within touch. The road is exquisitely kept, like all the streets of Calcutta, watered by bhistis with goat-skins perpetually, and perfectly hardened and levelled. In the cold weather, between the hours of four or five and seven, this course is thronged with vehicles of every description, — from the Viceroy's grand open carriage, with its smart adornments, its postilions, outriders, and body-guard of Lancers, down to the modest or immodest (for its unpretending driver is almost wholly innocent of clothes) ticca ghari, the Calcutta cab, or still lower, to the unassuming palanquin with its plebeian inmate. At the height of the cold weather — that is to say, in December — the drive is thronged; and the Row, or riding-course, beside it is alive with equestrians. After driving up and down the Strand, or the crowded part of it, a few times, one draws up at the gate of the Eden Gardens, where the band plays every evening. Philippa's carriage was always surrounded; for although everybody knew Barney Winterford, and most persons rated him at his true lack of value, his wife was always much sought after. She entertained incessantly, and one met the best people in her drawing-room and at her dinners. In India those two items are the essentials of success. Even social rank sinks before a well ordered kitchen and a well chosen list of guests. As for the gulf of indebtedness in the bottom of which the Winterfords wallowed, that was a social abyss too, and they found plenty of good company there. How far the tradesmen themselves are responsible for this state of affairs, it is perhaps unsafe or unfair to state. Certain it is that the redress which is in their hands is one of which they seldom take advantage. Men in both the army and civil service are encouraged to run in debt, and discouraged actually from its avoidance. The sons of peers, as the youngest of these men are apt to be, are known, or at any rate supposed, to have coffers somewhere in prospective ; and shadowy as these coffers may be, and dissoluble into thin vapor as they usually are, tradesmen are, as a rule, willing to place dependence upon those unreliable securities. Their customers are fashionable, at all events, and their shops are patronized by paying people — for there are a great many such — on that account. The Winterfords were highly connected on every side, and their patronage was in itself lucrative.

But a great change was working in Lady Barney. Her veins were throbbing, her heart was burning with indignation and impotence. She suffered Abdul to drive her up and down the Course, because

it was the custom, and she never in her maddest
moments had done anything unusual. She bowed
smilingly to everybody; but when Abdul drew up,
according to custom and even in response to her
order, at the gate of the gay Gardens, and she saw
Captain Stanhope dismounting from his horse, and
knew in a moment that he would be at her side, she
felt that she could not see him.

" Drive on, Abdul, to the Red Road ! "

The Red Road, so named from the color of its
soil, is a more retired drive across the Maidan,
or big grassy field, called the Lungs of Calcutta.
Across that she drove at last, through Chowringhee
and Ballygunge and Alipore, and back through
Alipore and Ballygunge and Chowringhee, just trying to collect herself sufficiently to think. Something, she knew, had to be done. What should
that something be ?

Poor, poor Philippa ! She had had for years a
feeling of shame whenever she complained even to
herself of Barney's recklessness, his utter disregard
of truth, his lack of moral responsibility. For it
had been all her own doing; for every moment
of unhappiness she had Philippa Winterford and
nobody else to blame. She had broken her father's heart, in marrying exactly counter to his
wishes. She had insisted upon joining her lot to
that of a jolly, fascinating, careless, young ne'er-
do-weel of an Irishman. What mattered it that he
held a title by courtesy? Scant courtesy it had
brought him in the way of favors from government;
and the fourth son of a rat-hunting, steeple-chasing

peer of Ireland, is not considered high game for the daughter of an English earl, equally impecunious though that nobleman be. It was a bad match; and Barney had borne out to the letter his irate old father-in-law's auguries. "Civil servant, indeed, and bound to get on, is he?" he said almost fiercely to his pleading daughter. "Old Munger-ford has never been out of debt yet, nor one of his sons. They have broken every bone in their disreputable bodies, racing; and there's not a wo-man in the family who has ever had a guinea to spend." And the Earl paced the floor in absolute anguish. But the Lady Philippa, loving her fa-ther desperately too, thought she loved Barney more; and pretty, piquant, and wilful, she made her father consent to the marriage his soul loathed. Her mother was dead.

Oh, that dear father! How more than noble and heroic he had been! How he had gathered the little flock of grandchildren, one after another, to himself! How stern he had been with himself, as well as with Philippa, when longing wildly to keep her, and to shield her from her wretched husband, he had always counselled her to go back to Calcutta with Barney. And even now that he had written her Ida's complaint, it was only for her honor's sake, and that of her children, that he wished their father to do something, no matter how little, for them. And what had Barney done? Yes, what had he done? Spent every penny he could lay his hands on, — betting, cards, racing, extravagances of all sorts. He had utterly failed as a man. Nobody looked up to him; nobody respected him; nobody loved him, but the children and Eileen and — herself; for Philippa did love him, — why, she could not say.

Then he never missed, or seemed to miss, their children. If Barney Winterford had once sat down, and burying his face in his hands, bemoaned the separation from his dear ones and hers, it would have covered a multitude of escapades in Philippa's eyes. But he hardly mentioned them much; and he appeared to take it for granted that other people would look after them and he had nothing to do but enjoy himself. " What good will my *not* enjoying myself do them?" he would ask, his blue eyes beaming with childlike wonder. " I 'll be the better father when I get to them, for keeping myself young, and not moping." So Barney grew younger, and Philippa older, every day. And the money grew less. Economy is unknown in India, and impossible; but it was not even economy Philippa had urged, only that he should use his salary in contributing something to his own family at home.

But this was not all Philippa was reviewing; here was Eileen, indulging in all sorts of whims, at their expense, — new Arabs to ride, new habits to ride them in, new driving-horses, carts, boxes of dresses out from Paris, and, most expensive of all, a disastrous order of flirtation with the wrong sort of men.

Then, last and worst, Barney had now deliberately lied to her, in words. It was not the first time he had deceived her, but it was the first time that she knew of his actually uttering a falsehood. Barney would have called it a good record; but to Philippa a direct lie was equal to ten subterfuges. It is so with many persons.

The alternative of leaving Barney, and going back to her father and their children in England, had, of course, often occurred to Philippa. It came to her in the form of a horrible temptation sometimes, but Philippa had always thrust it from her. Many wives whose husbands were in India lived apart from them; her children needed her every instant; their lives and characters were shaping themselves without a mother's guidance; their small aches and pains were suffered without a mother's soothing care. But Philippa knew that many wives could leave their husbands safely, trusting to those husbands to work their best, love and anxiety acting as spurs of the sharpest sort. She knew that leaving Barney in India would be the end of him. If she left him in anger, he would go to the dogs at once; if she left him simply upon the pretext that he would be less hampered without a household and would be able to come all the sooner to his family, he would never make an effort. He would promise, and perhaps go so far as to contemplate trying, but beyond an occasional visit, his family would never see him. Unless, indeed, he should be dismissed from the service for some misdemeanor, and come and quarter himself penniless upon the old Earl. He was quite capable of that. Whichever way she looked, there was nothing, — or at best, a high, black, blank wall. She longed to sail for England the next day. But how about the girl, Eileen, who was about as fit to look after herself as the Winterford baby? Well, Eileen was married, or had been, and should be able to take care of herself. A little discipline might be good for her. Philippa, you see, was hardening her heart very fast.

And so Philippa drove and drove, but came to no conclusion. She never drove so far nor so long. At last she found herself close beside the Nullah, or canal, shaded by palm and tamarind. Native boats were drawn up on the bank or glided lazily down the stream. It was dark now; and an old, old woman came tottering out from one of the thatched huts, bringing a little light, which she set upon the water. The tiny lamp bobbed and careened, righted itself, then floated steadily on for some seconds, when it suddenly came in contact with a stick. It tipped and was nearly extinguished; then the poor old crone, who was hobbling after with eager eyes, started and uttered a cry. Philippa sat quite breath-less, watching. It was steady again and burning well, with a clear flame. A heavier current ran against it, overwhelmed it, and out it went in an in-stant, without warning. A shriek now rent the air; for the old woman had offended the gods, and this was the test by which she could see whether or not she was forgiven. If the powers had smiled upon her, the light would have burned until the oil was spent; they were unpropitious, so it was put out and she with it into utter darkness. Her anguished cry lingered in Philippa's ears, as she drove on and left her crouching on the earth. Nothing Philippa could

have done or said would have comforted her; and
in truth, Philippa was in sore need of comfort herself. She came to a worse place next, — the burning
Ghaut, where well connected Hindus are cremated.
The flames darted high, and the smell of roasting
human flesh was in the air; the naked figures were
distinct against the blaze, as they danced and jumped
about the pile, while they heaped on the fagots.
Philippa turned her face away, sickened and disgusted. The drive had done her no good. There
was no help anywhere.

She suddenly recollected that they had guests to
come, and she should not be ready for them, — the
first time in her life she had committed a breach
of good breeding. The only thing she could determine upon was to have a " good long talk " with
Eileen, in the course of which she would deliver
some startling home-thrusts. It was thus the woman in her found relief. As for Barney, there was
nothing she could do to him; yes, she could preserve a freezing silence, when they were alone, which
would chafe him to frenzy, for Barney was an inces-
sant chatterer. And then she could refuse absolutely to entertain, on the score of extreme poverty.
No longer would she be a party to dishonor; for
the way they went on was simply, to use plain English, thieving. She herself would lead a life of strict
retirement after to-night, retrenching where she
could, and denying herself as many luxuries as
possible, without interfering with Barney's self-
indulgence. After all her excitement and desperation, however, she ordered the horses' heads turned

homeward, with the conviction that she was helpless and might as well abandon herself to a ruthless fate. She could make things a little unpleasant for Barney ; but he had his Clubs, and would live at them mostly, if she bored him.

4

EILEEN'S ride with Colonel Beverley had been one long triumphal trot, so to speak. She had ridden with him before, and was always the centre of admiration, wherever she went, in Calcutta, so graceful and so indifferent was she. But this had been a day when everything outward combined to make the Lady Eileen feel herself a power. The very air caressed her; it was the flower of the Indian cold weather. A little, a very little, bracing quality in the atmosphere; the last hour of a brilliant glorifying sun; a handsome, distinguished escort, and every eye in Calcutta upon her. A woman might scarcely wish more, and yet Eileen was unhappier than she had been for a long time. She had known for years that the moment when she allowed herself to be disgusted with her life would be the beginning of misery for her. The misery — faint and intangible, to be sure — had begun.

And yet my heroine, to whom acting, it would seem, was more natural than nature, was never so flushed and radiant as she appeared in the Row that day. They had galloped over the Maidan first, finding the Row crowded. Eileen, loving the exercise, as she loved nothing else, her exquisite face luminous and rosy, with the pure animal joy of it, was fairly magnificent; adding to her beauty of face her supple slender figure and her superb seat, the result was a marvellous moving picture. Everybody said, "Have you seen Lady Eileen Beaufort?" and those who did not approve of her stared at her most. When they went back to the Row, which was fuller than ever, they rode slowly and chatted; for the whole riding population was out, it seemed. As soon as the lamps in the Gardens were lighted, they got down and walked about; and there Captain Jack joined them, he flushed and radiant, too, with Eileen's success.

The Eden Gardens are lighted by clusters of lamps, like the Champs Élysées, and are prettily laid out; and here the band plays every evening early, and all the nationalities under the sun do congregate. Here are English, French, Germans, Spaniards, Italians, Russians, Greeks, Armenians, Jews of half-a-dozen sorts, Turks, Chinese, and every kind of Indians, pure and half breed. It is a bewildering, kaleidoscopic mass of color and light. There is no more cosmopolitan scene in the whole world, and certainly no gayer one.

There had been a Durbar in the morning, and twenty Rajahs and Maharajahs were driving up and down the Course, resplendent in the most brilliant hues and jewels. These potentates seldom walk in public; and there they are wise, for their legs are their weak points, — if what has length and length only can be called a point.

Close to the railing was a line of servants with
bird-cages taking a music-lesson of the band, — not
the servants, but the occupants of the cages. Every
horse had his syce or groom squatting at his fore-
legs or standing at his head or darting before him ;
and as the liveries were not of our sombre shades,
but as varied as the flowers of the field, if somewhat debased indeed from Nature's tints, the effect
was of rainbows upon rainbows, moving and darting and gleaming here, there, and everywhere.

Every man in Calcutta, it seemed to Eileen, had
come to talk and to walk with her ; sometimes their
group joined other groups, and they walked six or
eight or ten abreast, up the wide lawn and down,
and then the line would break up into pairs and trios
again. Colonel Beverley, instead of giving way to
the new-comer, clung to his post. He usually flitted
about like all the rest of the men, paying extravagant compliments, looking unutterable things. To-
day he sauntered on by Eileen's side, watching her
face narrowly, and admiring every movement. Ani-
mated always, she had never seemed so like mercury
to him. He did not feel for one moment that he
had her undivided notice ; and that fretted and galled
the proud chieftain, who was accustomed to slaying
his victims with those burning eyes. Eileen was
not more touched by his melting looks than she was
scorched by his fiery glances.

Jack Beverley reposed the most implicit confidence in the lady of his affections, — if she were not
honest, she would be nothing to him ; and so he
trusted in her truth as part of the unit he loved.

Lady Eileen had never rejected one advance of his ; modest as Jack was, he had to own that for some reason his ardor had been agreeable to her and therefore he was sure of her. Jack had inherited a very small sum from his mother. It was not enough to marry upon, but he had the prospect of an appointment soon ; and as soon as that matter was settled, was he not to lay that sum, with himself and his appointment, his honest heart and his clean hand, at her feet? And did not his father smile upon the whole affair? Was there ever, in short, such happiness ready at a man's call? He would have fought for it gladly, eagerly, — would have given his blood, drop by drop, for every smile, every touch ; and here he was, who had never deserved it, who had done nothing in his whole life, who could do nothing to begin to deserve it, actually at the height of his maddest ambition at one step. His eyes filled with tears, and his soul was full of thanksgiving.

Jack Beverley, in vulgar parlance, had been " born yesterday." He had been kept out of the world by a father who had no notion of figuring as a patriarch. He had learned a good deal of men at Aldershot ; but his experience of women, except at second-hand, was of the slightest, — limited to garrison belles, who, as every one knows, are more or less transparent in their wiles, and not so very fascinating, even to the inexpert. His vacations, from a small child, had all been spent at school and at the University by express command of his father, who wished to keep the boy unfledged as long as pos-

sible. But a manly nature helped him on, and
manly tutors taught him the right things; so Jack
had come out to India, brought up, as far as he
went, in the right way. To-night, happy and expect-
ant, as he approached Eileen, he saw a change in
her. Love had made him blind to her faults, but
he was keenly alert to her moods. She greeted him
sweetly, but without warmth. Eileen could be nothing but sweet — to him ; and yet there was — yes,
he noticed it more and more — there was a decided
difference in her manner, although Jack could have
hardly given it a name. It was a fine, subtle difference, and might not have been observed by any one
but a lover. The fellow tried to think of everything
he had done or had not done, or might have done
or might have left undone. He had lain awake all
night thinking of her, if that was a fault ; but that
could not be it, — she did not know that. He had
ridden at a respectful distance after her, keeping her
well in sight all that afternoon ; he doubted if she
knew that. Well, thank Heaven, he could have an
explanation and a conclusive talk with her before
another twenty-four hours had passed. They all had
engagements for that night, but in the morning —

This very misunderstanding, if it was a misunderstanding, startled him, and he made up his mind
to ask Eileen to marry him. He said to her, in
a voice full of emotion, unmistakably a lover's tone
and manner, — he meant it should be so, and Eileen
so understood it, — that he hoped to see her next
day early, and asked if ten o'clock would suit her.
Eileen replied graciously but not gayly, as was her

wont with Jack, that she should be ready to see
him at ten. The Colonel heard it, and bit his lip.
Jack, satisfied, changed the subject, and tried to
keep from leaping into the air and uttering loud
huzzahs.

Captain Beverley had not been mistaken. Eileen,
with the color mounting in her cheek, her fire of
repartee running high, was in a turmoil within. She
knew men well; and she had seen and recognized
and greeted with a ready response the truth and candor of this young fellow who was paying her such
devotion ; at least, she thought she had recognized it.
The devotion, Eileen had said to herself, meant
nothing to her or to him. It was boyish ardor,
and she had been brought up on that sort of thing ;
it was like her breath to her. As for love, it was
absurd, she said to herself perversely. Allowed
Jack's devotion? Why, yes, what of that? Her
conscience had never been trained. She had always
allowed men's devotion. Men were never the suf-
erers to begin with, she argued, — an indifferent man
was one she never looked at, nor spoke to, if she
could help it ; a man must be, or pretend to be,
absorbed in her, — a clever imitation would do, —
in order to interest her at all. Jack had been de-
liciously devoted, either really or feignedly so. Here
her false logic was, of course, put utterly to rout ; for
if it was Jack's candor which charmed her, how
could he have been feigning? The last day or two
the logic had been torn to shreds, and Eileen had
allowed her eyes to see, through the rents in it, that
Jack Beverley was in love with her. As for herself,

perhaps she was just the least bit in love with him. That very admission, slight as it was, had made her miserable, for her nature was so strange and wayward that she could not promise to be of one mind long.

That afternoon, during the ride, Colonel Beverley had planted a sting in her breast. He had grown confidential, and had spoken fondly and ardently of his son; but that son, he said, with a pained expression, had been the cause of much uneasiness to him. Jack had a way, it seemed, of devoting himself madly, heart and head, to a girl; and then, flinging her aside, of plunging quite as hotly into another affair of the heart and head. The fellow seemed to possess a kind of chronic susceptibility, his father said. He had tried to counsel him, — to show him how he was injuring not only himself, but the objects of his attention. "But the boy [Jack was twenty-three] has been so much away from me, and I know so little about training boys, that now he is quite beyond me; he is headstrong, and scorns my advice." The last victim ("Before me he means," thought Eileen, angrily) had been Sidney Markham, the Olmsteds' niece. Sidney Markham was a prim, pretty girl, whom Eileen had seen dancing and walking and riding with Jack, when she, Eileen, first came out, and before he knew her.

Eileen was much disturbed, but she changed the subject. Her respect and esteem for Colonel Beverley were largely the result of Jack's for his father. Jack had sounded his father's praises for hours together to her. She had rarely seen such perfect

regard. Sons in England, as a rule, are not abounding in veneration for fathers, and Eileen had remarked this extraordinary case many times. It
raised both men in her estimation. Now, why had
Colonel Beverley — a man of great dignity and family
pride, a man, too, whom she knew actually so little
— told her these things about his own son, unless
because he felt it his duty to warn her against that
son whom he, like everybody else in Calcutta, must
have seen to be devoting himself to her? The
Colonel was executing a difficult and a humiliating
task. He must, therefore, be sincere in this. This
ride was for the purpose of opening her eyes ; and
the Colonel's own admiring air must be to soften
the hardness of his words.

Eileen could not help being cold to Jack, even
although she was angry with herself for her clum-
siness. Why should she make a difference in her
manner, as if she had been mistaken in him and
cared?

Eileen chatted on now, as if nothing in the world
were troubling her. The Lieutenant-Governor and
his party had joined theirs, and they all sat down on
one of the benches. There were some ladies with
the Lieutenant-Governor, and some other men, and
they were all talking about the Durbar in the
morning.

"I met a Maharajah," said Eileen, laughing, to
Sir Apleigh Eaton. "His name was Puttiala, and
he was very gorgeous, also extremely disagreeable.
He wore some of the Empress Eugénie's jewels in
his turban, and he had a tassel of brilliants depend-

ing exactly over his right eye. I could think of
nothing but the jargon we speak to our servants, and
insulted his Royal Highness by using the contemp-
tuous *tum* instead of *ap*. I was too confused to
know what to say. After I had struggled with a
long, choice sentence and been worsted, he answered me in Shakspearian English ! "

" Oh, all those men speak English," laughed Sir
Apleigh, — " all those who were here to-day. You
ought to meet Jeypore ; he is really a most cultivated
man, and interesting too."

" How is Sindhia? " asked Mrs. Brabazon, one of
the party. " He is my hero."

" Puttiala is mine," said Eileen, laughing. " He
stared at me, and apparently considered me a solemn
object. Is he profound? "

" No," answered Sir Apleigh ; " he is dissipated,
and not at all a good sort of man."

" What does one talk about with natives? " asked
Mrs. Brabazon. " I often have to entertain them,
and never can find a theme. Your learned and
interesting Jeypore called my attention to the efful-
gence or refulgence of the waxlights in the chande-
lier, and descanted upon that. I never know what
subjects to broach with them."

" They are interested in inventions, and in topics
of general interest somewhat," said Sir Apleigh ;
" in English and Indian politics, some of them, in
science, in metaphysics. They don't know much
about fashion, it 's true. Of course they vary according to taste ; and they have not the social art
of concealing or changing their interests to suit their

company. A good many of them are very curious
about our sentiments and opinions."

"If the truth were told, they are too deep for us,
I suppose," said Eileen. "They think, and we don't.
What a tonic it would be to meet them all the time
for a few months, — to be obliged to drop personali-
ties, and talk upon real questions of the day ! "

"It would not be a tonic, in the sense of an
appetite-creator," laughed Colonel Beverley, who
had never taken his eyes off Eileen's face, "if one
had to live with them. Their ways of living are
horrible. I have been a bear-leader ; I know."

"What is a bear-leader?" asked one of the
ladies of the party, who had just come out from
England.

"It is a person who travels with a dancing bear,"
said Colonel Beverley, "and sometimes the bear
won't dance. In other words, my dear Mrs. Stuart-
Kendal, it is an English resident at the court of a
native prince. If a man survives that, he can stand
anything."

It was growing dark and late, and the Gardens
were nearly deserted now. The Winterfords' carriage, which was always at the gate, had not been
seen there, although one of the suite had been
despatched every few minutes to look for it.

"I can't walk home in my habit," said Eileen,
aghast. "It's too far, and so late too. I shall have
to come to a ticca for the first time in my life ; nearly
all the carriages have gone."

"How stupid of me to send the horses away ! "
exclaimed Colonel Beverley ; "but I made sure of

Lady Barney's being here.   She never misses coming
to the Gardens."

"My horse is here," Jack broke in; "but, of
course, a lady can't ride him with my saddle."

"Nor unattended either," said the Colonel, crossly,
in an aside to his son.   "Why do you mention ab-
surdities?   Get the best-looking ticca you can find,
for Heaven's sake!   I never was so mortified in my
life," he said, turning to Eileen.

Jack came bounding back.   "Blessed be native
stupidity for once!" he cried.   "Your men mistook
the order, and Lady Eileen's horse is waiting.   You
take mine, father!"   And Jack raised his hat, and
walked off to prevent discussion.

Barney met the equestrians at the gate of his own
house.   He was driving.

"Why, Barney," called out Eileen, reining up.
"You are surely not starting out at this hour.   Everybody has left the Gardens.   It's time to dress for
dinner."

"I'm going for a turn," said Barney.   "I've had
no airing.   It's hot, and there's no party to-night,
and Philippa's not come in from driving.   Dinner
will not be until nine."

"Oh, horrid!" cried Eileen.   "It's only half-
past seven and I'm starving.   How unkind of you,
Barney, to change the hour without consulting us!
Besides, Barney," and her eyes opened wide, "there
is a party; the Strahans and the Olmsteds are
coming to dinner.   Do you suppose I could forget
such a prospect?   Why, Barney, you're off your
head."

Barney looked startled. "Good gracious !" he said, "you 're right, Eileen. But where 's Philippa, then? She never drives as late as this !" And Barney, with a remembrance of his wife's last lofty look, really turned a trifle pale in the dark.

"Why, I don't know," Eileen said. "At home, I supposed. And yet it seemed odd; she always comes to the Gardens or sends the carriage for me."

"I will ride out and look for her," Colonel Beverley offered, with a show of concern.

"No, no," said Barney. "Thank you, Bev, I 'll go myself. Philippa has driven a long way, I suppose, without thinking." It was a thing she never did. "I only hope that brute of a coachman had not had too much arrak. Go in, Eileen," he said, seeing her anxious look. "Nothing is wrong, of course. We lead such ridiculously regular lives here that the least deviation upsets one."

Barney, in turn indignant and indifferent with his wife, had laid a small plan of his own, which was now forgotten in his vague alarm. He had intended to go out driving himself, and to stay out late enough to make Philippa very anxious. Then, after she had worried a good hour or so, by which time he should have been very hungry, he was to come home; and Philippa, in her joy to see him, would have forgiven and forgotten everything. Their own dinners were the best in Calcutta, and Barney rarely stayed away from one of them.

Philippa, all unconscious of the hour, had turned the tables upon Barney at his own game. He would

not have dreamed of worrying, if it had not been for
the scorn and anger with which she had left him.
There was nothing she could do; and Philippa was
not the person to " do " anything.   Yet he was perturbed, and he had a faint presentiment of evil.   So
it was a great relief, after he had scoured the roads
about, to see Philippa's carriage coming into the
little street at one end as he entered it at the other.

The house-servants were standing about in the
driveway, which was unwonted for them.   Eileen,
in dinner-dress, was pacing the veranda nervously.
Altogether there was an air of disturbance about the
house.   Philippa pretended not to notice it.   Barney
drove in just behind Philippa, and rushed to help her
out.   Make up your mind, Philippa, what shall it be?
Reserve, anger, indifference, concealed suffering, —
what?   Proud reserve it should be, thought Philippa, and above all, silence.   No arguments, no
threats, no pleas.   Disdain, I am afraid it was, but
she called it reserve.

" Why, Flip," Barney said tenderly, as he handed
her out, " how you have frightened us !   Where on
earth have you been? "

" Just driving," answered Philippa, stepping out
leisurely.

" Driving at this hour by yourself is not safe," he
urged.   " Don't do it again, dear ! "   His show of
solicitude moved Philippa to more anger than she
had felt before ; her cheek flushed, and she walked
in a stately manner up the stairway, to be met by
another perturbed spirit at the top.

" Philippa ! " Eileen exclaimed, on the landing.

" How naughty of you to frighten us so ! Barney
has been out looking for you ever so long."

Philippa smiled coldly. " I 've been for rather
a long drive," she said. " Did you go to the
Gardens? I forgot about your riding. How did
you get back?"

" I managed," said Eileen ; " or my syce did for
me, by misunderstanding the order to go home,
luckily. It 's pretty late, and your dinner-people
will be here in twenty minutes." Philippa vanished. She had no idea of being rude to her
guests, and was shocked at her own tardiness.

CHAPTER VI.

THE Strahans were high up in the civil service, and had to be conciliated. The Hon. Alexander Hope Strahan was a tall, severe-looking man, with long gray whiskers and no mustache. His eyes were small and colorless; his lips were thin and firmly set. He disapproved most strongly of Barney Winterford, personally, as did Mrs. Strahan of Eileen. Lady Barney, somehow, commanded respect. She, although as remote from brilliancy as can be well conceived, — and in fact brilliancy would not have been in her favor with that set, — was dignified and decorous, and no one in Calcutta had ever one word to say in her dispraise. Even the men who voted her an icicle found her steady and useful as a chaperone and a friend, if they needed one. She was a woman whom no one knew intimately; and not to be known intimately is in itself to be respected.

Mrs. Strahan was little, and plain, faded, and rather dingy. She had large, pale blue eyes, and a large smile; the eyes never darkened, — it was not their fault, poor things! they had no facilities, — and the smile was fixed. She sang, in the usual amateur drawing-room voice, and drew in a mincing way. It was the popular impression that she was clever,

and most persons were afraid of her. Next year her
eldest daughter was to be brought out, and that was
one reason why Mrs. Strahan showed open hostility
to Eileen. The Olmsteds and their niece Sidney
Markham were also at the dinner; a Judge of the
High Court and his wife, — sweet serene people,
wrapped up in each other, and one in all things, including an intense desire to get back to England as
soon as possible. Sidney Markham was stiff and
quiet; she had dovelike eyes and a sweet smile.
She was very pretty, very conventional, and very
easily shocked. It was just the party to bring out
Eileen's worst points, and to-night she seemed possessed to air them all.

There were two extra men of the party also,— Tom
Carbury, to keep Barney in countenance; and Sir
William Mann, a member of the Viceroy's Council.
Lady Barney was not distinguished for the congruity
of her dinner arrangements.

She was out before any of her guests arrived, after
all. She moved restlessly about, adjusting a vase
here, straightening a table-cover there, and at last
she sat down at the piano and hummed softly for fear
of conversation with Barney. The Olmsteds came
first; and while Philippa and Mrs. Olmsted were discussing the next tea and the last novel, Eileen and
Sidney Markham were trying to carry on a girl's talk,
— dreary, for the heart of neither was in it. Barney
and Mr. Olmsted were talking about matters at
home, and appointments and recalls in India; and
then Tom Carbury with the Strahans entered the
room, and the conversation became more general.

5

There were two coals, or perhaps three, in the drawing-room grate ; and the punkahs having been re-
moved, one felt that winter had really set in. So
Eileen said laughingly to the Hon. Alexander Hope,
who was standing, with his back to the two coals,
in true English home-fashion.

" Do you remember Punch's remark, ' Summer
has set in with its usual severity ' ? " Eileen asked
Sidney Markham and Mr. Strahan, who was standing
by them. " I always think of it when we play at
winter here. Once I do remember drawing the
curtains and huddling up close to this mean little
grate, and once — no, yes, could it have been? —
yes, I did, — I positively shivered ! "

Mr. Strahan looked solemnly at her. " I think
our evenings are really cold in December," he said.
" I wear a fur coat when I go to the opera."

" There is a chill in the evening air," replied
Sidney.

" It 's smoke and dampness," said Eileen, perversely. " There 's nothing so chilly as smoke."

Philippa, who expected to pass a dreadful evening
with Eileen and these people, looked up, and tried
to convey a warning glance. Eileen knew too much
to look at her and went on. " That sealskin coat of
yours is painted to imitate fur, — now own it ! " she
said, looking at the Hon. Alexander Hope. " It 's
made of muslin really ; you can't deceive me."

Mr. Strahan smiled in a sickly fashion. He never
knew what to say in response to a joke.

Sidney Markham looked bored. " I wear furs,"
she said, " all through the cold weather."

"Another subject, quick!" thought Eileen; "this
one is done for. — Speaking of operas," she asked
suddenly, "what *are* our operas to be this cold
weather?"

"Third-rate Italian this year," broke in Tom Carbury, offering Eileen his arm, at a signal from Lady
Barney. "Last year it was fourth-rate German;
next year it will be fifth-rate French. What bad
music one does put up with in India, to be sure, and
what hags and patriarchs one has to sing it!"

"Why is it?" asked Eileen. "Why can't we
have, say, second-rate talent at least? We have
never soared as high as that yet, have we?"

The Strahans had been always foremost in bringing opera to Calcutta. Mrs. Strahan, who was seating
herself next but one to Eileen, overheard this and
bristled. "I wish those who think it a simple matter
to import opera troupes would try it," she said with
acerbity. "We have had all we want of drudgery
and ingratitude."

"You have done beautifully," broke in Mrs.
Olmsted, with a smile; "I'm sure no one has
complained."

"Oh, yes," said Mrs. Strahan, "we hear our com-
panies called third and fourth rate constantly."

Eileen, who loved a brush with Mrs. Strahan,
was opening her mouth, when Mrs. Olmsted spoke.
"The difficulties are well known," she said. "No
first-rate voices will come to the East. The voyage
is too trying, and the climate; and then getting
out of the country is so doubtful! We have had
two managers, you know, absconding with the sub-

scription money, and leaving the poor wretches to beg their way back to Europe. Shall you ever forget," she said, turning to Philippa, " those pitiful things, and the way they hung about for months? Some of them, I am sure, are here now."

" *I* never shall forget them," said Barney, sighing. " I used to shut my eyes, going round corners on my way to my office, for fear I should see an elderly *ingénue* or an aged *coryphée* begging for money to get home with. Pickett married one of them, you know, to get rid of her. Some of them were not so lucky."

It is not often a dinner of ten becomes so social, and perhaps Philippa thought Barney would better devote himself to two persons at a time; so she began a low dialogue with Mr. Olmsted on her right, and for a time general conversation died.

Captain Carbury and Eileen were friends, and they might have had a jovial dinner of it, if it had not been for Mrs. Strahan, on Tom's left. Mr. Olmsted was busy with Lady Barney a part of the time, and then Eileen would remind Captain Carbury of his duty to Mrs. Strahan; and once or twice that lady herself broke in upon Eileen's and Tom's talk. Once Eileen was saying, " I don't know why it is that women are always so mortally ashamed, so afraid, of having it known that men have treated them ill."

" It is because," said Mrs. Strahan, with a flush, " it means disgrace."

" I don't agree with you at all," said Eileen, " if you will excuse me. When a man jilts a girl, if *I* were the girl, I should far rather the truth would be known. I should be a thousand times more ashamed of throwing a man over than of being thrown over by him."

"How dreadful!" exclaimed Mrs. Strahan, with a horrified look. "It is a lasting disgrace to a girl to be 'jilted,' as you call it."

"You would think so too, Eileen, if it were your case," suggested Philippa, shaking her head surreptitiously at Eileen, who tossed hers in reply. There was no use in airing out-of-the-way sentiments before these people. They understood only cut-and-dried opinions and ways of thinking.

"On the contrary," responded the Irrepressible, boldly, and in rather a loud tone, "a man did once treat me very ill."

"How old were you?" asked Barney, dryly. "Six or seven? You were married before you were out of pinafores."

"Oh, I was old," answered Eileen, — "old enough, that is to say, to feel it a good deal. He jilted me. I am not joking, truly."

Barney and Captain Carbury were the only ones at the table who enjoyed this. Philippa thought remarks of the sort in wretched form, Mrs. Strahan was utterly horrified, Sidney Markham looked silly; and the others could not understand joking, if it was joking, upon such a solemn subject. Captain Carbury laughed aloud.

"You are the most amusing woman I've ever seen in my life," he whispered to Eileen, "and the women who say those things are the ones

who are most beset by men.   Much a man jilted
you ! "

"A man," said Eileen, soberly, and looking full
at Carbury, "paid me conspicuous and devoted attention, followed me about, made desperate love
to me, in short; and when I thought he was going
to ask me to marry him — and I had every right to
suppose it — he did n't !   I found that he was car-
rying on the same performance with other women;
that his honesty was the best kind of acting; that
his impassionate utterances were drama of the first
order.   I suppose it is a common thing; it happened to be my first experience of the kind.   I do
not mind; I am not ashamed.   I was hurt and angry,
but I don't think I was in love, and I don't think
I suffered, except in my self-esteem; and that was
the last rag of it,— I have none left, not a shred."

"That was not jilting, surely," said Captain Carbury.   "I don't believe you know what the word
means.   The poor fellow saw, before it was too late,
that there was no chance for him; and if you were
not touched, Lady Eileen, you must have had
a good deal of amusement and an easy escape.
Most men are not shaken off so easily.   He perhaps
knew you could not be won, from the first.   But I
believe, from what I know of the man — "   Eileen
turned pale.   "No, no," he said, "I beg your
pardon; I do not know that man, of course.   I only
mean from what you say of him, and from what
I have seen of you, that he had to flee in time,
or to be burned to a crisp at your shrine.   Every
man I know is afraid to see too much of you."

"I fancied," said Eileen, growing suddenly red, and looking down, "that we were talking truth and sense. I loathe flattery; I abhor the kind of thing you have just said. You don't believe me, I dare say; you do not know me."

Eileen turned away from Carbury, angry with him, with herself, with everybody. She had been natural and ingenuous just to see what the effect would be. It had ended, as everything else did, in a fulsome compliment. Everybody thought that was what she expected and needed, and must have. Bah!

Sir William Mann had been talking temperance and early hours and good habits generally to Sidney Markham. Not that she needed suggestions on these points; she was exemplary to a degree. But she was a good listener; so they had got on very well. Eileen now joined in. "Then you believe in shutting up shops — I don't mean shops, but eating-places, restaurants, early at night, Sir William?" said Eileen. "What are poor, hungry theatre-goers to do then?"

"I'm afraid poor, starving theatre-goers would have to sup at home, or go without," said Sir William, smiling down upon Eileen; and Eileen, with the crimson flush in her cheek, in her pale blue dress, with the candle-light upon her, was something to smile upon. "I disapprove of this eating in public, which seems to have proved so fascinating of late years to our people. It is entirely un-English, to begin with, and I certainly disapprove of keeping the worn-out men and women who have to be at their posts early next day up to unheard-of hours of the night. It is barbarous."

"Oh, if you come to that," said Barney, "nobody wants to work. Everybody is tired. If you sup late at home, you keep your own servants up; and as for making coachmen and footmen wait out in the cold all night, why, think how we have to do it in England! And if we spare our own servants, as some persons do, and hire livery-men, why, there's the same cruelty again. One could have no service at all, if one stopped to think of servants' fatigues all the time."

"I never thought about the waiters at restaurants, poor things!" said Eileen, pensively, and rather ignoring Barney's remark. The new turn in the conversation had attracted listeners; and seeing Mrs. Strahan's pale eyes upon her, Eileen went on to her destruction. "I remember once being put out of a restaurant in London at midnight by the police." (Philippa positively gasped, and Barney looked severely for once at his sister. "Is the girl mad?" he thought.) "You were with me, Barney, I think, or perhaps it was papa; at any rate, it was a man, of course, — it doesn't matter who." ("I should think it did matter who," remarked Philippa. Mrs. Olmsted had a serious notion of marching Sidney Markham out of hearing of these extraordinary reminiscences.) "Yes, it was papa," laughed Eileen. "How frightened you look, Philippa! We walked into this place calmly and unsuspectingly, after the theatre, ordered our supper, and were just eating it, — most delicious oysters, or something, — when a

policeman came in, if you please, and ordered us
out. You may imagine papa's language," said
Eileen, turning to Barney. " If it had not been for
me, he would have fought the whole police force
(my relations have tried that sort of thing before) ;
but I made him come out quietly, although I was
furious too at having my supper spoiled. But I do
remember now how tired the poor thing looked who
was waiting upon us, — ready to drop. I 'm glad
he got to bed a little earlier, if one did lose one's
oysters."

There was nothing very reprehensible in what
Eileen had been saying ; but Philippa, who had
heard something startling from her sister-in-law
every time she had heard anything, and who saw that
most of her prim guests were neither amused nor
edified, was thankful when the dinner ended. Philippa was hopelessly depressed in mind, body, and
spirit ; and although she had seemed as usual, it was
with the greatest difficulty that she had been civil to
her guests. And Eileen did nothing but say shocking things, and injure herself with important persons
in Calcutta, whose favor might mean much to her.
Poor Philippa ! she felt even more indignation with
Eileen than with Barney at the moment, and was
glad to give the signal to withdraw.

It was not very lively in the drawing-room after
dinner. They talked of a young wife who had been
sent home in disgrace for flirting, of a new engagement, an old divorce. Eileen and Sidney talked of
tennis and their horses and the next Government
House ball. The question of trains or no trains at

the next Drawing-room was a subject which was absorbing the population feminine of Calcutta just then, and that was discussed in all its bearings. Jack Beverley's name was mentioned, casually, by somebody; and Sidney blushed.

"I hope I did not blush," thought Eileen. "I know I did not. I can conceal everything I feel, I am glad to say. It is a great art."

"We are going to England in March," said Mrs. Strahan, "quite unexpectedly. My husband applied for leave, for his health, but we really hardly expected to get it."

"Does Milly come out with you?" asked Sidney Markham.

"Yes, she will come out for next cold weather. She is a tall, handsome child."

"Is she like her father?" said Eileen.

"My own family is tall," said Mrs. Strahan, not looking at Eileen, as she bit off the words, "and there have been some celebrated beauties in it. How hard it must be for you, dear Lady Barney," she said in an undertone a minute later, "to look after a headstrong creature like that! She must be frightful to manage."

Philippa flushed. The angrier she was with Barney, and the readier to scold Eileen, the more she constituted herself the outward champion of both. "I find no difficulty in guiding her," she said with a smile, which had a kind of hauteur about it, — a combination for which Philippa was noted. The exact point at which the freeze melted and the thaw congealed, nobody knew. But it was

an effective process, and Mrs. Strahan said no
more.

The custom of sitting over wine had almost gone
out at the period of which I write, although old-
fashioned people, like the Strahans and Olmsteds,
who detested innovation, still clung to it. Out of
deference to them, therefore, Barney kept his guests
a quarter of an hour after the ladies had gone up.
But Tom Carbury stayed hardly five minutes. Eileen
had a new and strange charm for him to-night. He
perhaps was one of the very men of whom he had
himself spoken, — those who had dared see little of
such a priestess, — but he felt drawn to her to-night,
particularly as he remembered that he had offended
her. Eileen was sitting in the corner of a high-
backed sofa, with her feet on a cushion. Her dress
was of a blue so pale that it was nearly white, except
in folds where the shadows made color. There was
soft lace about it, and she was sitting in the simplest
attitude a young woman can take, and the hardest
to take gracefully, — her hands were lying in her lap,
and her head was thrown slightly back. She did
not stir as Carbury approached her, nor smile, nor
make room for him. So he went and sat beside
Sidney Markham, and looked at Eileen.

Later, when the other men came upstairs, Tom
went and stood behind her. He leaned over her
sofa. She did not look then. "I'm sorry," he
murmured softly, "very sorry." Eileen did not
move. "Whether you forgive me or not, I am still
sorry," he said.

"If you are sorry, then," exclaimed Eileen, suddenly, sitting upright, and looking over her shoulder at him, "come here and talk to me like a rational being. Tell me why life is so empty when people like these are by. Why can I not smile and be gracious and yet distant, like Philippa? And why would n't I be, if I could? Why do good, stupid persons, who are worth a hundred of me *apiece*, bore me to the verge of shrieking? And why do I show the worst in me, and shock them, and hate them, and let them all see it? Don't tell me they are not stupid on account of their goodness; I know that, or at least I should know it, I have been told so enough. What do you think, honestly?"

All this was rather beyond Tom, who had never analyzed a sensation in his life. But he recognized, with true manly instinct, that a fellow-creature, and a beautiful one, was suffering the pangs of self-disgust. He had come to her side long before this, and was sitting on the couch by her. "I am forbidden to make fine speeches," he said, "so I cannot tell you what I truly think. You have never learned perhaps to get the best out of people. I suppose many can do that. I eat my dinner, and thank God for a good one. I enjoy the lively guests, and let the dull ones alone as much as possible. Then I go home and forget the stupid parts of the evenings and dwell on the bright ones. That 's all the philosophy I have. I try not to offend these prim creatures; perhaps you are too young to have learned that. It does n't pay, you know. You oblige me to speak roughly. Now, if I said what I really felt, I should — "

"No, you would n't," interrupted Eileen, smiling brightly upon him. "You are good to me, and I forgive you now and thank you. I will tell you something. I am worthless, I know nothing, I care about nothing, I make nothing of my life, I make nothing of others' lives. This looks like penitence, does n't it? and I suppose you think it 's a hopeful sign ; but it is not even that. It 's only a fit; it won't last. I shall be just as bad to-morrow ; in fact, I am just as bad now. But I don't want you, nor anybody, to think that I don't know what a fool I am, — that 's all."

Mrs. Strahan was singing ballads ; Sir William Mann was turning over the music for her. After she had sung her two songs, with ten verses each (the regulation number), Sir William, contrary to all precedent, urged her to sing again. She simpered, and complied with the request. Her style evidently suited him, for after even the third ditty he clapped his hands gleefully together, and exclaimed, "Oh, more, more ! "

"Why," exclaimed Eileen, "Sir William, you are as bad as Oliver Twist ! "

"Was Oliver fond of music? " asked the august member of Council, innocently.

Tom Carbury was flattered by Eileen's confidence, but he need not have been ; for Eileen that night would have confided in anybody who could understand her language. And Carbury was the only person in the house who had a ray of intelligence, she said to herself impatiently. Philippa would have called this disgust of herself vulgar, — I don't

think Eileen understood Philippa.   Barney would
have roared at her and called her silly.   The Olmsteds
and Strahans and Sidney Markham and Sir William
Mann — well, he might have looked upon her as a
convert, to be sure, and hailed her symptoms with
joy, but the rest would have gaped at her in dismay.
Mrs. Olmsted would have given her a soothing drink,
and put her to bed perhaps; but the Strahans, —
oh, what was the use of even thinking of them !
They never entered into her calculations for a moment, except on an occasion like this.

They sat, Eileen and Carbury, ostensibly listening
to the song, but really waiting for an opportunity to
go on with their talk.

Tom spoke when there was a chance. " I 'm glad
you have said this to me," he said, " and I 'm awfully obliged to you.   You shall speak of it first, if
you like, or not at all when we meet again.   I sha'n't
allude to it.   It is only women who are everything, who speak of themselves as nothing." This
was very eloquent for poor Tom, and he grew very
red.   " If I had any ambition, I should feel as you
do all the time.   Jack Beverley does feel so. ' Here
am I,' he said to me only to-day, ' a great, strong,
hulking man, leading a flunkey's life ; when for a
good mount, comfortable quarters, pretty clothes, and
a French *chef,* I settle down into a fool's Paradise,
and let life and all its obligations go over my head.
I tell you, Carbury,' he said, ' this India can be so
much, and is so little, to us English.   What do we
know of the lives of these miserable wretches about
us?'   I think, Lady Eileen, that it was our little

talk under the banyan-tree this morning which started you both out in such a doleful strain."

Eileen looked happy. It pleased her to hear Captain Carbury speak in that interested way of Jack Beverley, even although she could no longer believe in him. What a pity it was about that susceptibility of his ! she thought. He had so many good points, and was so superior to all the other men out here !

"What are you two ranting about?" broke in Barney at this moment. "Eileen, for Heaven's sake, let one of those 'grimmers' [Barney's name for stern officials] talk to you. You are awfully selfish."

Tom frowned. "Don't, Barney ! " he said, " your sister has been only too good to me in letting me keep her here all this time ; and as I see the fair Strahan making her adieus, I will say good-night to Lady Barney."

"'Good-night,'" mocked Barney; "what ails you, Tommy? Are n't you going to stop and talk over this bewitching evening with me? I want to talk to you about a lot of things."

But Philippa motioned to Barney, and he was obliged to go. Carbury hurried away. He would not stay and chatter now. He was a lazy, indifferent fellow, but only from habit ; and Eileen had awakened something in him which had lain asleep for a long time. He was, for the first time in years, going home to think. If a personality bore a prominent position in his thinking, the thinking in itself was a great advance.

CHAPTER VII

EILEEN BEAUFORT did not even know that she had fascinated Captain Carbury, — particularly, that is. She was full of uncertainty that night, and was not dreaming of conquest. She was ashamed of herself for being piqued with Jack Beverley, when, as she repeatedly said to herself, she did not care for him, and did not mean to marry him, of course. The prospect of the interview in the morning was rather perplexing to her. "Why is he coming," she said, "if he is treating me badly? And why am I not glad he has deserted me? Because I thought he was the first true man I had ever seen," she answered herself. "Therefore I must needs wish him for a footstool. I wish I knew what I did want. If I only knew something to wish for, it would be an improvement." Eileen leaned her head wearily against the sofa-cushion. After bidding the guests good-night, she had sat down as she was sitting before.

"Will you ask an informal lot in for to-morrow night, Philippa?" Barney asked, coming back to the drawing-room, as his wife was disappearing. "I want something to take the taste of this out of my mouth. The Bedloes and Veseys and Brabazon, and perhaps Stanhope, or Beverley, or Jack. Carbury is a good fellow, but those others! Oh, why should we undergo such grinding torments? They don't like us and never will; and as for you, Eileen — "

Philippa interrupted him. " I shall ask no one," she said grimly. " I have given my last dinner in Calcutta."

Barney stared at her in amazement. " Your 'last dinner'!" he repeated. " What do you mean by those tragic accents and that solemn phrase? Are you going to die?"

" I have decided not to entertain," replied Philippa. " We need not discuss the point. Eileen, will you come to my dressing-room?"

Barney's eyes positively glared. " What under the sun — " he began, and stopped. " Neither will I discuss the point. We'll eat our dinners, and ask our friends to eat our dinners, as long as I am the master of this house!"

" Will you come, Eileen?" repeated Philippa, as if she heard not.

Barney fairly flung himself from the room and into the veranda. He was nearer real anger than he had ever been in his life, against Philippa; and to tell the truth, it was a sudden turn for a long-suffering wife of seventeen years' standing to take.

Eileen followed Philippa, looking a little scared. Was a crisis coming in all their lives? Philippa sat down before her dressing-glass mechanically; and the ayah, her ankle and arm bangles tinkling as she walked, began to take the pins from her mistress's hair. Philippa looked so handsome, so regal in the candle-light, the red roses on her breast giving her a flush, her eyes bright with excitement, her lips quivering with the effort just made, — for Philippa was at heart gentle, — that Eileen lay on the flowered couch, gazing admiringly at her. Neither of the women spoke until Eileen, slipping from the couch, threw herself at her sister's feet, and clasping her knees, looked up into the stern face.

"Don't!" said Philippa, almost crossly.

"What is it, dear?" asked Eileen. "What has happened to trouble you to-day? Tell me; let me be something to you."

Philippa had not known of Eileen's inward struggles, — how should she? Eileen, always wild and incorrigible, had certainly not shown much desire for self-improvement that evening. Besides, Philippa was just then too much engrossed by her own misery to notice any change in Eileen. Eileen was always sweet and affectionate to her, or usually so. The beautiful face looked beseechingly into the face which had once been beautiful, and an imploring look filled the upturned eyes. "If only," she thought, "while I am in this mood, I can be of some service to somebody!" But Philippa was too grimly miserable to be stirred much, even by Eileen's appealing look. There was nothing to say about herself, nothing to be done. Her husband had simply turned out — turned out? he had always been — worthless. It was not an original grievance; a great many husbands had done the same. And there was nothing picturesque in her situation. She

was not young ; nobody cared for middle-aged misery. And besides she had not called Eileen in for
that, but to talk seriously to the girl herself. It
was hard to begin with that girl, already melted at
her feet. It was impossible, she felt, to begin as she
had intended. She must make an explanation first ;
so, being full of her own grievance, she glided into that.

"Eileen," she said at last, with a painful effort,
"I'm sure you do not know what a spendthrift
Barney is. He throws away every penny he earns.
He is over head and ears in debt ; he does nothing
for his own children, and that is why I will give no
more dinners. You see that I am right."

"Yes," said Eileen, softly. "Barney cannot help
being a spendthrift, — we are all so ; but we can
help encouraging him, Philippa." Here she laid her
small hand upon the other's, and spoke abruptly,
"Am I a worry to you?"

Philippa turned away her head. Eileen was certainly lovely, and so innocent in her sins ! What
should she say? "Yes, you are, Eileen," turning
her head, that she might not see the other's sweet
face. "You are a great worry to me. You spend a
great deal of money ; you flirt like a school-girl, and
you shock people horribly with your wild ways. I
speak the truth to you, since you ask it. I am
beside myself sometimes when I see you, and know
what a penniless lot we are, and how this must all
sooner or later end."

"Do you want me to go away, Philippa?" Eileen
asked, her eyes full of glistening tears, some of sorrow
and some of anger.

" No ; I want you to marry Mr. Warwick," answered Lady Barney, looking full at Eileen, who hid her head in the folds of her sister's gown. " I do not ask you to make a great sacrifice of yourself. He is not old ; he adores you, and — "

" I do not love him," said Eileen, in a low tone, not looking up. " That sounds babyish, I suppose, and is, of course, nothing in the way of my marrying him." There was something unspeakably sad in the world-worn look which came over the fresh young face at these words. " But the trouble is, I like him very much."

" There," said Philippa, brightening, and taking the face in her hand, raising it in spite of itself, " I knew you did not dislike him. Then why can you not marry him ? "

" Because," said Eileen, — " because I like him very much." Then after a pause she added, " If I did not like him, I might marry him."

" I suppose these are called subtleties," said Philippa, drawing her hand away and shutting her eyes wearily. " I confess I do not understand them."

" Philippa," said Eileen, resting her head upon her sister's knee, " I could not make a sacrifice ; it would be impossible, because I have nothing to give up. If Mr. Warwick were not the kind of man he is, I would agree to make him miserable, for your sake and Barney's. I have no conscience, particularly, but I could not bestow myself upon him and see his life ruined. I could not, indeed. He has been too kind to me. I will write him the truth, if you like; and if he wants me under such circumstances to marry him, I will do so."

"Of course," answered Philippa, "putting it in that way is equivalent to refusing. As for my sake and Barney's, you know very well that you wrong me, at least, when you say that. You are in our charge, and it has come to this that we cannot look after you any longer, unless you will help yourself. Mr. Warwick came to see me to-day about you. He says you fill his thoughts; he cannot give up the idea of possessing you. He is a fine man, and not a *parvenu;* he is well enough looking, and rich beyond words, and he will make you a perfect husband."

"That comes last, of course," said Eileen, with proud disdain. "I will write him, Philippa, but I shall tell him the truth; and if he wants this rare bargain, he may have it. Perhaps if he knew it was going begging, he would not care so much for it. Still, he's a simple soul, and his liking will last. I deserve my fate, Philippa; I shall not cry out against it. I know I have led a selfish life, although there has been precious little pleasure in it, and that I have made myself." Eileen was standing now, and moving toward the door. "If Mr. Warwick does not want me," she said wearily, "I dare say I can stay here until papa sends me money enough to take me to Ireland."

"Have I deserved this?" cried Philippa, seizing the girl's hand and drawing her back by main force. "I cannot sustain you in luxury any more, but it is only because I cannot sustain myself in it. My last

crust is yours, Eileen, and you know it; but an end
is coming to the crusts.   Some change has got to
be made, and I am thinking of you entirely when I
urge your marrying a man who will look after you
handsomely to the end of your days.   Do you think
I do not *writhe* at having to make this petty wretched
money the theme of my whole existence?   Do you
think I do not hate the pride which makes it impossible for me to go out as a servant, and earn my
children's bread with my own hands?"

Was this Philippa?   Eileen threw her arms round
Philippa's neck, in a sudden revulsion of feeling.   She
was eager to seize upon the favorable moment; for a
glimpse of the pent-up woman in her sister had never
been granted her before, and she was starving for
sympathy.   But the opportunity fled.   The haughty,
self-repressed Philippa was already ashamed of her
emotion, and with an almost rough movement she
disentangled Eileen's arms.   Eileen, now that the
vista had once opened, was not immediately discouraged, however.   She drew Philippa down on
the couch, to sit beside her.   " Why don't you talk
seriously to Barney?" she said gently.

" Talk to him !" echoed Philippa, her lip curling.
" For seventeen years, it seems to me, I have done
nothing but talk to Barney; and I have told him
that he is ruining his children's lives and his own,
not to speak of the trifling circumstance of breaking
my heart.   He does n't care, Eileen.   He loves you,
I think, — not to the extent of making any sacrifice
for you, perhaps, — but his affection for you is greater
than anything he feels.   I simply fret and bore him,

because I can no longer laugh at follies which in a
man of his age are crimes. It is a vital point with
me, and a stupendous joke with him, that our children have no dependence upon their parents, and
that we are disgracefully in debt. If Barney were
to come into one large fortune to make ducks and
drakes of, and another were tied up for me and the
children, we might live bearably while his held out.
There is no use in saying all this to you, Eileen,
except as an explanation of what you think is extreme harshness to you."

"Never mind me!" cried Eileen. "Barney
does love you; he does, he does," she exclaimed.
"You shall not say that. He was born careless,
brought up carelessly, and will die careless. My
father is the same; I am the same; Terence and
Ulick are the same. Barney should never have
married. I 've often heard papa say so. Philippa, I
shall speak to him. He does not realize what he is
doing, and perhaps if I let him see that I know — "

Philippa recited the episode of the fourteen hundred rupees to Eileen. "What do you think now?"
she said. "Will talking do good to such a man?
No, Eileen, I shall make no more pleas, certainly
none through you. You 'd better go to bed now.
You have your future in your own hands, and if you
do not choose to take it, I shall say nothing more.
I 'm sorry to have been betrayed into so much vulgar temper." And she held out her hand in her
usual formal fashion. Eileen went so far as to kiss
the cold cheek timidly. She did not dare attempt
to make a further demonstration. No one could

pierce that icy coating, when the surface had frozen over.

Eileen went downstairs and found Barney in the dining-room, smoking and playing Patience. A long tumbler of whiskey and soda was beside him, and his anger was apparently appeased, for he looked up at Eileen and laughed. "Well," he said, "it's dull times for the old man, when he has to make shift with himself for a partner. I say, Eileen, what did Flip want of you? By Jove, what a mood that woman's been in to-day! It's more than flesh and blood can stand."

Eileen smiled, but faintly. She had been too long on rollicking terms with Barney to change her base suddenly; yet a solemn purpose was firing her. She laid her hand upon her brother's arm. "Come up in the veranda, Barney, out into the air. I want to talk to you."

"Talk! Let's not talk; I'm tired of talk. Let's play écarté, if we do anything."

"Come!" said Eileen. Her face was so earnest that Barney looked up into it with a kind of comic gravity, like a monkey.

"Whatever's up?" he asked. "Tears, as I live, in the girl's eyes, and such a scarey, scolding face! And Philippa in a grand, stagey, Lady Macbeth temper! I know what's the matter with her; she'll be all right after a night's sleep. But this bonny little thing in its sulks! Faith, I don't know what to make of that!"

"Don't, Barney!" said Eileen, really distressed. This sort of thing was so new to her and so thor-

oughly out of her line ! And she did love Barney,
and alas ! was so in sympathy with him.

"Don't scold me if I go with you, will you?"
said Barney, getting up and yawning, yet gazing at
her in mock supplication.

"Come !" she said. After all, how much more
agreeable and amusing the bad ones are than the
good, thought this naughty person. She did not
realize at the moment that there would be no
danger in them if they were not. Satan in
horns and hoofs would repel at once. It is Satan
in cap and bells and in wreathed smiles who
fascinates.

When they were seated, or recumbent rather,
on lounging-chairs, and Barney had had his peg re-
plenished, and a fresh cheroot had been lighted,
Eileen cleared her throat ominously.

"Gracious !" ejaculated Barney, turning to look
at her. "A sermon !"

But the long chair was not suited to Eileen's purpose. She could never be severe in that attitude.
So she got up and sat in a straighter one. "Barney," said she finally, in a trembling voice, "do
you know that you are ruining nine lives by your
course?" Eileen meant his own life, and his
wife's, and those of their seven children ; but it was
an unfortunate beginning.

Barney burst into a loud peal of laughter, which
stung Philippa, grieving in her chamber.

"Am I a cat then?" he asked. "I have broken
nine bones in my body steeple-chasing, but each of
those was not a life, was it? What are you talking

about, stupid little girl, eh?" And he laughed again and looked wonderingly at Eileen.

"You have seven children," said Eileen, slightly daunted by her false step. "You have not forgotten their number, I suppose? and you have Philippa, and you have yourself."

"And I have you," broke in Barney, still gazing at Eileen with a look in which curiosity and disdain were equally mingled; "and faith, I'm afraid I sha'n't have you long, for your reason seems to be tottering."

"You are making every one of those lives wretched, indeed you are, Barney," Eileen went on, ignoring the interruption.

Barney laughed nervously. It was not very amusing, for all that. "Now, my girl," he said, sitting up and looking full at Eileen, "I understand this whole affair. You are primed. Philippa's been coaching you. There's something the matter with her, and she must needs contaminate you. I never saw two women so changed. You need n't say any more, Eileen, — no, not one word!" for Eileen's lips were beginning to move. "I've had enough of hysterical women for one bout. Only remember this: I'm not to be meddled with, nor advised by children like you; so go to bed and take that to your heart and keep it." And Barney stalked angrily through the long drawing-room, down the stairway and out.

Eileen stood for a few minutes, gazing into the soft starry night. The perfumes of citron and orange oppressed her, and the sweet-scented jasmine was stifling. She had not made much by her somewhat theatrical move, but even that was not troubling her most. She did go to bed at last, but it was not Philippa nor Barney nor Mr. Warwick who haunted her dreams. Through them all she saw, first in one face and then in another, but always gazing reproachfully at her, the great dark eyes of Jack Beverley.

CHAPTER VIII.

A WOMAN who can be described in a few words is not worth describing. If her complexities blend and infuse so harmoniously — like the primary colors — as to make what we call simplicity, — the white of the spectrum, — she is the most artistic, the most successful artistically of beings, also the most womanly. If she is simple, actually, — that is to say, either blue or green, or violet or red, — she may be pretty and sweet and lovable, or horrid, ungainly, peevish, but she will not be worth much as a study. I doubt if a book could be written about her. And the question is, Would she be a real woman? The height of simplicity is the concealment of art. Jack Beverley was simple, or rather, *simplex;* he never could have been a hero by himself, in our modern acceptation of the word.

I have read lately that the mysteriousness of the soft sex is a tradition only; and that women are as easy to understand as men (honest creatures!), if only one did not blind one's capability of understanding them by presupposing them to be darkly complex. These opinions, coming from one of our keenest pens, made a decided impression; but that impression was

shortly afterward blurred by reading a story of
the same writer's into which he introduces women
most irrelevant and unreasoning, — the most feminine of their sex, in short, — and makes remarks
about them like these : " Who knows what is in a
woman ? How many moods in a quarter of an hour ?
And which is the characteristic one ? " His first
utterances were in the nature of an essay ; his story
was life. Woman is complex and contradictory ;
and everybody who knows anything, knows that.

My heroine, Lady Eileen Beaufort, fulfilled these
requisites of complexness and contradictoriness in a
supreme degree. She herself went so far as to say
that she woke up in the morning with an entirely
new set of traits from those she had taken to bed
with her the night before ; and I go so far as to believe that the old ones were obscured for the time
being.

A great many things had occurred in Eileen's
life to form strengths in her character. The powers
were working in the dark, and the " splendid pat-
tern " that they wove " their wistful hands between,"
had as yet taken on neither form nor semblance.
Throw an arithmetic and a grammar and a geography
at a child's head, and keep on pelting him with books
of learning, and I doubt if he will come out edu-
cated. Eileen had never learned her alphabet yet.
The lessons of life had all been hurled at her ;
she had not slowly assimilated or digested one.
She had never yet known the desire to know, which
is the A B C of acquirement.

Eileen had tumbled up in Ireland ; her childhood

had been lawless and wild. She had broken in horses principally, and had been indulged to excess by a doting father and adoring brothers. (Barney had married when she was a small child, and her mother had died at her birth.) An aunt in London provided conventional gowns three or four times a year, so that Eileen was fashionably attired without knowing it, and at eighteen she was sent to the aunt for a season in London. The season had been short and severe. Captain Beaufort — the fastest man in England, and the wickedest — had fallen — pitched headlong into the most desperate kind of so-called love (why is our vocabulary, rich in unnecessary nomenclature, so poor here?) ; at all events, an excellent imitation of that much abused passion, more like the original than the original itself, transfiguring himself temporarily and enveloping its object. It might have burned itself out in a short time, this white heat, or cooled, so that one could have discerned the real metal, had not the anxious aunt — anxious with a cause, poor soul ! — telegraphed the alarming condition of things to Lord Mungerford, the father, who came speeding down from Tipperary; and Barney and Philippa, who were luckily just departing for Calcutta, bore the girl secretly from the very jaws of the feverish Captain.

Eileen, who was more overwhelmed than conquered by the Captain's mad wooing, made the best of her position, and took to the gay life in India as a duck takes to the water. She was making conquests by the score, when Beaufort — whom

Overland Routes could not daunt, nor P. & O. steamships destroy — appeared in Calcutta, and, fair means failing, resorted to foul, and absolutely forced Eileen to elope with him. He was cashiered the army for gambling ; his passion burned itself out ; he brought every kind of disgrace upon his young wife. Disgrace could not taint her nature, however, for she did not perceive it. She did not know, far away in a small watering-place on the Continent, that her husband was suspected and dishonored, for they were living among people who had no right to enlighten her. She accepted her fate, not meekly, but with airy fortitude, and thought she was learning the lesson of life. Yet her true nature was never touched. It remained gay and light and sound and sweet after a year of horrible discomfort. When she discovered that her husband loved nothing but drink and dice, she was relieved rather as regarded herself, because she felt she owed him small duty in the way of wifely affection. When Beaufort was killed in a bout, — an orgy of three days ending in a fight, — Eileen was terrified and anguished much as a child might be ; and although for years she could not shut out certain terrible sights with which that season was filled, little of the truth reached her, through the kindness of those whose hearts she had won, and her father's coming and seizing her from her surroundings before she had time to realize the facts. It all seemed like a figment of a disordered dream.

Eileen stayed with her father in Ireland for two or three years. She had become more serious and sober, and read a good deal, and imbibed some cynicism, but was otherwise outwardly not much changed. In three years Lord Mungerford felt that the affair had blown over, and that Eileen, with her bitter experience in mind, might be trusted to see the world again and to make a wiser choice. But the aunt would have none of her. The wild alarm and frightful anxiety of Eileen's first season would never " blow over " with her, and she declined gently, but firmly, to become a raving maniac again, for anybody's sake. So Eileen stayed in London at Philippa's father's house in Eccleston Square, " looking after " Barney's children, she said, and " trying to feel that she was of some use in the world."

Eileen was a little wild yet for a perfect guide to the young; and the boys somehow were engaged in more escapades than they had ever indulged in in their lives before, and in fewer elevating pursuits. Young Barney, at this period, lured a London cabby from his box, and seizing the reins, drove wildly through the crowded streets, bringing up ignominiously against a lamp-post and smashing twenty pounds' worth of property. He was horsewhipped by the frenzied cabman, too, and cursed loudly on the public highway; and as his grandfather had the mortification of his disgrace to bear, and also the annoyance of disbursement, Eileen, who, she herself now nobly allowed, had in a moment of impulse suggested the wild step to the boy, was voted by the old Earl, not unnaturally, to be an improper adviser for his grandson.

The old gentleman wrote Philippa that she was *impossible.* "What is to become of her, I don't know. The bogs of Ireland are the only place for her. She is so pretty and so girlish, so amiable too, except for a peppery spirit, which burns itself out in two or three wild flickers, that it is extremely hard to be severe with her. I confess myself wholly unequal to the task of managing her, and to tell the truth, I cannot see my own responsibility in the matter. Having been married, she cannot be disciplined or even chaperoned; and her widowhood is the most incongruous thing about her. She is a kind of monstrosity viewed in that light, for anybody so distinctly unwidowed I never have seen. She is very gay at dinners and At Homes and balls now, and of course her career is canvassed everywhere, — particularly I have no doubt at those cankers of civilization known as luncheon-parties. It is not very agreeable having her affairs raked up again, and it will be hard for her to marry well here, in spite of her beauty, with such a record. Barney and Ulick madly love her, but she is not a safe companion for them. Don't you think it would be better for Barney to write his father to take her home? I can't suggest it very well. Dear, dear!"

Philippa told Barney, of course; and Barney immediately insisted upon having her out in India again. This was how she came to be there a second time.

CHAPTER IX

TO fascinate was Eileen's fate. She had rare charms of person, of bearing, and of manner; she was bursting with spirits, which nothing could extinguish, it seemed. Philippa's position went far toward reinstating Eileen's. Everybody in Calcutta bowed at Philippa's shrine, and society there is so migratory that after three or four years there were not many who knew personally of Eileen's past. Philippa's conscience had never ceased to prick her for the negligence of which the men — her father and brothers — had been guilty toward the only girl in the Winterford family; and she honestly tried to do her duty by Eileen, as she conceived it. But her duty, as she conceived it, was not to teach or to tame or to employ the strange nature, which, to tell the truth, she but dimly understood, but to marry it off to a rich man with the greatest possible speed.

The morning after Eileen had promised Philippa to write Mr. Warwick, she had remained in her room, and had seen nobody. She expected Jack Beverley, as we know. That interview would not alter the state of the case now. She was to marry Mr. Warwick, if he would take her on the terms she offered. She had already refused him three times, and the last time he had gone away promising never to trouble her again. Now she would trouble him. Eileen was not yet safely started on the right road; but she was earnest and sincere this time on the wrong one. She wrote : —

MY DEAR MR. WARWICK, — You will be surprised at this note. It is going to be a strange one, and I may not be able to express myself at all. I like you very much, although I do not, and never can, love you. Will you take me for your wife under those conditions? I ought to tell you, of course, that my reason for changing my mind is a financial one. That sounds and looks so base that I hardly dare send such insolence to a man like yourself. Alas! it is true. I await your reply.

Yours, in all candor, EILEEN BEAUFORT.

The answer came, long before Eileen expected it, in the person of Mr. Warwick himself, — pale as a ghost, with sad eyes and trembling lips. He was hurt, cut to the quick; but his love for Eileen was so great that it was not even affected by the indignity put upon him. He was a good, honest, middle-class Englishman, — a man who had made his fortune in banking, and who had never been unscrupulous. He was considered a great catch by the mothers of the nobility even; was rather handsome, very dignified, a little bald, and a little inclined to be stout.

Eileen drew aside the red curtain of her boudoir, and came into the drawing-room with a faltering step. A realizing sense of her presumption now overwhelmed her. She had been impulsive and had given way to her impulses so long that she could hardly grasp the situation even now, — that she had insulted a man who had offered her his best, his all, and that she was in his presence. She hesitated in the doorway, not daring to advance. Her eyes were cast down, her face was bright crimson.

Mr. Warwick felt his heart bound and rebound, and then sink like lead into an abyss from which it could never be recalled; but he went quickly to her, and led her gently to a seat. She did not look at him. Mr. Warwick tried to speak. "What did you think I would do?" he asked huskily. "Did you think I loved you so little that I would accept your sacrifice, and see you pine and die in your chains?" (If she thought he would refuse, then why subject herself to this humiliation?)

Eileen sank on the floor, and covered her face with her hands. "You said last week," she murmured, "that whether I loved you or liked you or hated you or were indifferent to you, you wanted to marry me. You said that to see me was joy enough. I told you I did not love you; you said that was no matter, if I loved no one else."

Mr. Warwick smiled bitterly. "I did say all that; I meant it. But I did not want you to marry me for financial reasons alone."

There could be no other, Eileen was on the point of saying; but she checked herself, and put it in another way quite as insulting. "If I had yielded then, what would have been my reason?" she asked, taking courage and removing her hand, yet still looking down. She might as well make herself as bad as she could. "I said I did not love you,

I said I did not wish to marry you. You kept on
urging me. If I had yielded, what would have
been the reason? "

Mr. Warwick smiled sadly. " I fancied," he said,
not without a touch of pride, " that my devotion
might have gone for something ; but I was wrong,
of course. I thought I might teach you to love me
in time."

" No," burst in Eileen ; " it is all nonsense to believe that love comes after marriage. I am poor
and have lived long enough upon my family, which
is poorer than I. I might help them and you, and
lead a useful, perhaps a happy life. But if I have
mortally offended you, and I know I must have
done so — "

Mr. Warwick stooped and lifted her to his side.
" Oh, my child," he said, " my child, I do love you
so, and I did long to guide that flaming spirit of
yours ! But I am using all my strength now to
thrust you away from me. I would not let you
marry for money alone, my child ; it is an awful
fate. I wish I could give you my whole fortune,
and see you enjoy it ; but that, in this censorious
world of ours, would not do. You must promise to let
me know if you are ever in need of anything ; and if
there is something I can do now, perhaps — " Eileen
shuddered. " I believe there is difference enough
in our ages for me to do it without comment."

Eileen grasped his hand, and pressed it ; but she
shook with shame all the time, and not once had
she lifted her eyes to Mr. Warwick's. " Why can't
I love him? " she thought. " He is the best man I

have ever seen. I don't believe I have ever seen a really unselfish one before." Suddenly, and like the bursting of flame, she looked up into Mr. War- wick's face. "Perhaps I can love you!" she said joyously. "I think I feel it coming. I never liked you so much, certainly."

Mr. Warwick flushed with pain, and tears came into his eyes. "Dearest girl!" he said, and thrust her gently from him. He could not bear the strain another moment. It was harder every instant to give up this extraordinary treasure. Once he turned after he had started to go, and kneeling, kissed her hands; then he walked quickly away.

Eileen sat dazed. To her this man would always appear with a halo round his head. And she — she, worthless coquette, she said, could not love this saint; and Barney had contemptuously called him a "business man"!

At last Eileen got up wearily, and crossing the drawing-room, tapped at Philippa's door. The bad things might as well all be got over at once now. The next in order was to tell Philippa of this inter- view, and after that to go through an equally painful one with Jack Beverley, who, strange to say, although it was twelve o'clock, had not yet come; for whether he asked her to marry him or not, she could not help remembering with pangs the words of the Colonel his father.

Philippa opened the door herself. She was very pale, and held a note in her hand. The note was from Barney, and announced that he had gone pig- sticking, and had no idea when he should be back, —

perhaps in a week, perhaps not for a month! He hoped he should find some rational comfort in his family when he came back; and when their senses had returned, they might pen him a line (giving a remote address). He was sure to do or say something disagreeable if he stayed now, as he was much annoyed; so he took himself off.

Philippa took the note back from Eileen's limp hand when she had read it. She did not speak.

" It's a joke, of course," said Eileen, — " a ghastly one, but still a joke. Have you asked the servants?"

" Oh!" said Philippa, " it was not necessary to do that. I knew he was about something. The bearers were stirring all night downstairs, and Barney too, I dare say. I have not seen him at all. I heard him drive off this morning too."

They stood, the two women, for some time without a sound. Finally Philippa turned to leave the room. She spoke over her shoulder. " You 've had Mr. Warwick here?" she said.

" Yes," answered Eileen, "he has been here. I asked him to marry me, and he refused." Eileen was ashamed of her flippant tone, but she did not know really how to express herself.

" You put it, no doubt, on the ground of our poverty?" sneered Philippa, turning half round and glaring angrily at Eileen.

" No, dear," said Eileen, gently, throwing her arms around Philippa's neck, " but on the ground of my own. I could not do otherwise."

" Knowing, of course," retorted the almost distracted woman, "that there was nothing for him to

do, but to 'refuse' you, as you coarsely express it.
One more of your unconventional, extraordinary
performances; that's all. I can imagine just how
dramatic and ridiculous you made yourself." And
Philippa, who had shaken off Eileen's arms at the
beginning of her speech, beside herself at her own
troubles, and only too glad of an excuse to be
violently angry with somebody, dashed into her
bedroom.

Events were happening with a rush in the Winterford family. Eileen was beginning to live; and life
so far was frightfully unpleasant.

CHAPTER X.

THE following week Philippa spent in preparing for a voyage to England, — home, — never to come back any more. This last act of Barney's had driven her to a decided step. It was so cowardly, so cruel, that she seemed to find no vestige of manliness in him; and she could not, would not, feel herself bound to stand by him any longer. The preparations were made quietly, and even Eileen was not told.

Everything but Philippa's own personal belongings was to be left, so that there was not much bustle necessary. "Why should I trouble myself to look after things?" said Philippa. "Let the master of the house attend to his own affairs. I have done." She even felt a kind of malicious glee in wondering how a man who had never had one domestic care in his life would manage under the circumstances.

Of course, Philippa's conscience pricked her about Eileen. It seemed cruel to leave her behind, and still more cruel not to tell her; but Philippa was transformed, distorted by her wrongs. She saw everything with lurid, savage eyes. Barney had never in his life done this kind of thing before. With all his carelessness and extravagance, he had

never been brutal to her personally. Now he had
gone away, for no one knew how long, leaving
her absolutely without money and with perplexing
financial difficulties. Philippa had no intimate
friends in Calcutta, and she would appeal to no
one. She sent her own brougham and country-
bred horse to the stables, and the price they fetched
would pay her passage home to England. She
paid visits, went out to luncheon, drove, chatted as
always, and preserved a proud equanimity. She
did not mention the coming trip, for fear Eileen,
and perhaps Barney, indirectly should hear of it.
After she had gone, it mattered not what people
said; she should never, never see India again, and
Barney might bear the brunt of gossip. It was high
time he bore something.

It was difficult to know what Barney's thoughts
were at this crisis, or if he had any. After seventeen years of absolute, colt-like freedom, a man
could hardly be brought up with a tight rein and a
stiff harness in a minute. He chafed and champed,
I may say, at such a sudden and unexpected round
turn. He had always done what he liked; and Philippa, although she had never gone so far as to like
it too, had borne what he chose to do. Why had
she not taken this stand when they were first married? "Egad! if she had, she never would have
come out of England with me!" thought Barney,
chuckling at his own savage pleasantry, She had
never had any money; neither had he. What did
she want money for? She had always been clothed
rather expensively, had lived in rather handsome

houses, had given and eaten good dinners, had plenty of friends. Debts need not worry her; he had to bear the brunt of those. On the whole, he began to feel that he had given his wife a pretty easy time, as times go. It was degrading, of course, to talk so much and fret so much over the everlasting wherewithal, which was so vulgar and yet so important. "But that's what this row is about," Barney soliloquized. "In fact," he added, "it's the unfortunate and unlooked-for incident of my having a little money, by Jove, that has parted us! Well, I'll go back next week, and Flip will make up, she will be so glad to see the good-for-nothing old man safe again. If she won't, why, let her go. I can amuse myself without her. It will be dull at home, of course. Philippa has made things bright, dear old girl!" and then a tear would actually steal into the miscreant's eye, and trickle down his cheek. But he was roaring with laughter the moment afterward, and had forgotten wife, home, everything, — he would have forgotten his children, only he had not thought of them in that connection, — at some sally of Stanhope's; for Stanhope was outdoing himself in jollity and good-fellowship.

Eileen seemed to have more engagements than usual during this week, and had been out a good part of the time. All day Saturday she was busy in her room, and Saturday afternoon she announced to Philippa that she was going to Barrackpore with the Viceroy's party for Sunday. At this Philippa turned pale. Her own plan had been to spend the next day *tête-à-tête* with Eileen and to tell her, —

for Sunday would be too late for demurral or objection to have weight, — and to arrange that Eileen should stay with a Mrs. Granby — an elderly woman who had been a friend of Eileen's mother — until Barney came back; then, if Eileen and Barney chose to keep house together, they could do so. It was none of Philippa's affair. Well, she would write her a long letter on Sunday, explaining everything; and whether Eileen judged her harshly, or everybody judged her harshly, or not, nothing mattered now. She would be the solace of her father's declining years and the stay of her own dear children.

Once the thought did come to her, — what if Biddy, darling, sweet little Biddy, come to Eileen's age, herself dead and Barney in charge, should marry as Eileen had done, and be left as Eileen had been, a young widow? Philippa gasped; but her grim resolution was taken, her wrongs must be avenged.

She kissed Eileen affectionately, put her arms about her neck, and the tears did gather in her eyes. Her resolution weakened, but she spurred herself on by thinking of her bitter wrongs.

"It will be dull for you, darling, and I hate to leave you," said Eileen, fondly. Philippa shuddered. "But I am obliged to make this little visit. There are reasons which I will explain to you on Monday." Poor Philippa! She could not utter a sound. How Eileen would hate her when she found that she had deliberately deceived her!

Eileen detached herself from her sister's arms.

" On Monday, then, dear," she said, and went away.
If Philippa could have seen what Eileen had been
doing in her room, if she had heard the directions
given to the servants, and if she could have observed the look, sly and sad too, which came into
Eileen's eyes, she would not have been so sure
that her own secrecy had been so wonderfully
maintained.

Philippa stood near the door, lost in a confusion
of thoughts. Riotous, mad, ugly thoughts they were,
new and unwonted for that gentle spirit. Revenge
was uppermost. Even the " dear children's " images
were visible to her mind in a kind of halo of fury.
The picture of Barney returning, gay, careless, full
of apologies, confident of finding his wife anxious,
alarmed, and consequently ready to forgive as always,
— Barney coming to his house to find her gone,
— what joy she felt in the prospect of so circum-
venting him ! All her regret at her conduct toward
poor Eileen was swallowed up in this grim joy.
Poor Philippa ! Her eyes were of steel and her
lips of white lead, as she dragged herself to her
lonely dinner. She busied herself Saturday evening
by destroying all her letters. On Sunday she went
to church as usual ; but the strain was too great
there, and she came out " feeling faint," she explained to the person next her. " Forgive us our
trespasses as we forgive them that trespass against
us." The words choked Philippa, who in whatever angry frame she had gone to church before,
had always melted and forgiven Barney everything
at those words ; for Philippa meant every word

she uttered, in prayer and out. The gentle petition excited her to frenzy. She knew she could not reason against it. Of course it was her duty to forgive, she knew, but she could not see her duty then in the whirlwind which surrounded it; so she went home, nursing her wrath all the way.

She was in terror all day, for fear Barney would appear. He might be in Calcutta all the time; she knew nothing of his movements, but at all events the thing was a dead secret. Her ayah knew that she was going away, and perhaps one or two of the bearers; but until the boxes went on the following morning to the steamer, not a soul would know, and it would be too late for even Barney to stop her then.

After church various men came to pay visits, as is the custom. Philippa saw them all. Yes, Barney was off with Captain Stanhope. Her manner had always been languid and indifferent concerning her husband's movements, so she had not much to affect now. Pig-sticking? Yes, she believed they had gone pig-sticking. Coming back? Oh, she did n't know. "Whenever the pigs stopped biting," she laughed. Fred Barnet, who was calling, said afterward he had never known the icicle in such a melting mood; she was even droll, and made jokes!

All the afternoon it took to write Eileen. Then there was a short drive, a shorter dinner, a long evening, a wakeful night, dawn, and the early start.

CHAPTER XI.

EILEEN had had a hard week of it. Captain Jack Beverley had disappeared, without a word or a sign. The last time she had seen him was that evening when she had ridden with Colonel Beverley in the Row. He had asked, with great earnestness, — which was feigned, of course, — if he might see her the next day, and that was all. He had not come, he had not sent. He had not been seen.

Colonel Beverley had been kind and thoughtful, and really devoted to her. Eileen supposed he thought her moping for his wretched son. She would let him see that no such thought disturbed her. Jack went off a day or two ago, he said. Calcutta was getting too hot for him. He did not explain what Jack had done, of course ; but he implied that it had something to do with Sidney Markham.

It was while she was in this state that she discovered Philippa's secret. It seemed a pitiful thing to Eileen, — this lame and ineffectual attempt at concealment. Eileen was sure ; and to make assurance double, she had gone to the P. & O. Steamer Office and found " P. W.'s " cabin engaged. It was a simple matter to engage one for " E. B." near it.

For Eileen's mind was made up to leave India.
She was wasting her life here. She must go to England with Philippa, and be of service to her. She
had only hampered and hindered Philippa heretofore ; now all that should be changed. And Eileen's
sparkling face took on a sober, fixed look, as she
vowed to be nothing but a drudge — forever.

The Sunday at Barrackpore helped Eileen out
immensely in her machinations. She must come
into Calcutta Sunday night by train, stay with Mrs.
Gillespie, the military secretary's wife, over night,
confide in her at that late moment (that was the
worst of it), go on board early, and hide in her own
cabin until the vessel was under way. It was a bold
plot ; and Eileen was nervous and excited all day
Sunday. She had never been quite so gay. The
men were all at her feet. There were all the aides,
gay, dashing, young captains, and there were visitors
from England, and there was Colonel Beverley, whom
Eileen had not expected to see, and whose presence
embarassed her somewhat. At luncheon she sat at
the Viceroy's right hand, and he devoted himself to
her ; devouring her beauty with his large, round
black eyes, set close together and hedging in his
large aquiline nose in a manner that suggested
a bird of prey, and was not altogether pleasant to
the objects of his admiration. His compliments
were fulsome ; and Eileen was always glad when a
prettier woman than she appeared, and released her
from these blushing honors.

" We are to have an operetta in two weeks," said
the Viceroy, " and you are to take a part. It is to

be the 'Crimson Scarf,' and you are Tessa. The costume will suit you perfectly; all that network of velvet skirts, you know, and the pretty Venetian head-dress. I see you in it now."

"You do more than others will, then," said Eileen, with a laugh. "I cannot do the part, truly," she uttered. "I pray your Honor's clemency; give it to Sidney Markham."

The Viceregal brow clouded; its owner was not accustomed to contradiction in his absolute dictatorship at Calcutta. "I hoped my request was a command," he said pettishly; "it is usually so considered. I have given out that the Lady Eileen Beaufort is to do Tessa. We can't possibly do without you. I pray you to reconsider this freak." The Viceroy's ill-humor alarmed the others at the table, who hastened to amuse and interest him.

"We 've got a first-rate artist to paint Moonbeam [his favorite horse]," broke in Captain Carbury, — "a man who was just passing through Calcutta, and glad to do it."

The august host looked through the daring interrupter, and turned completely round, facing Eileen. "My wishes in this matter seem to me reasonable," he said in a low tone. "You will offend me mortally by refusing to grant them."

Eileen looked pathetically childlike, as she raised her eyes imploringly to his birdlike countenance. "There are good reasons," she returned, in a tone as low; "you will know them to-morrow. — And how sly and horrid you will think me too!" was her mental addition to the remark.

8

The Viceroy showed his annoyance so plainly
that Eileen was a little uncomfortable. "Have me
bastinadoed," she laughed, tossing her head, "for a
bad subject."

"For an incorrigible, disobedient piece of wilful
loveliness," rejoined his Viceregal Majesty, half smiling and half cross. "I know you will reconsider and
do my behest. Come, I ask it as a favor. Is it possible you can resist an appeal like that?"

"I would do it, if I could; but I can't," Eileen
said decidedly; and then reflecting that she should
be off in the morning, she added defiantly, "This is
my ultimatum."

The Viceroy was so seriously vexed that he left
the table.

Colonel Beverley strolled by Eileen's side to the
cool, dark morning-room. Eileen was not anxious
to be alone with him. It had troubled her rather
to find him at Barrackpore. And yet he was such a
noble, fine man that Eileen felt, after all, that he was
about the only stanch friend she had in India, except
Mr. Warwick. "How unreliable first judgments are!"
she said to herself. "I could have sworn at first that
Jack was far the better man of the two. A fig for
perception!" They sat down on a low sofa near
the long windows. Hedges of scarlet pointzettia
glowed in the sunlight. The day was perfection.

"You are looking lovely, dear Lady Ellen," said
the Colonel, gallantly. "Are you tired of hearing
that? It was the first thing that rose to my lips, I
assure you. It is useless to try to think of anything
else with that face before one."

It was the worst course the Colonel could have chosen. Eileen was in no mood for trivialities; and barefaced compliment always angered her.

"You must know me little, and respect me less," she said, gazing angrily at her admiring companion, " if you think that sort of thing pleases me. I want to be serious; I want to live. I 'm trying to shape a course. You hinder instead of helping me when you make me feel like a simpering wax-doll. No, never mind disclaiming," she said hastily, for Colonel Beverley was about to break in. " Don't apologize, nor say anything more of the same sort. I loathe compliments of the kind men give me. The highest flattery would be to consult me about some important question, — something that is of value, of weight."

The Colonel sat looking on, highly diverted. He had resumed his easy attitude, and was watching every turn of the pretty head, every turn of the proud lip. She never looked so lovely, he thought. The new rôle suited her better than any other. `

He looked fondly upon her. " Forgive me," he said softly, tenderly, " I spoke from impulse entirely. Your beauty is inward as well as outward; no one appreciates that fact better than I. Common compliments are vulgar, and I am ashamed. — Most women like them," he added to himself; " how is one to know? — Truly," he went on earnestly, " I know you are in perplexity. Can I be of the slightest service? Pardon me for saying that Barney is frightfully thoughtless, and that I understand how much worry he is giving you both."

Eileen started. She might almost confide in Colonel Beverley; he would help her, and after she and Philippa were gone, he would have an eye to Barney, at all events. But, no, a man like Colonel Beverley, wise, strong, deliberate, would certainly oppose her scheme, and call it girlish, headstrong. She dared not tell him.

It was impossible to leave Calcutta forever without learning something more definite about Jack. She might ask quite calmly now, and not appear to pine for him. "Did you say Captain Beverley had gone for very long?" she asked, with an assumed air of carelessness.

"No," answered Colonel Beverley, with a slight flush. He was unprepared. ("How sensitive he is about that boy!" thought Eileen; "I am sorry I have distressed him.") "No, he has gone to the Mofussil, I hardly know where or why. He made some excuse about shooting, or visiting chummeries, or something. He is an odd chap. With every appearance of an infant's candor, he is really as deep as a well."

"He has always seemed straightforward and honest to me," answered Eileen. "I am often mistaken in faces, but I hardly thought I could be in his. However," she added hastily and laughingly, "I have not made a study of his physiognomy, and might easily be wrong. There is one thing I have not quite understood" (this rather timidly). "He made an appointment with me for the morning after he left. It was not an important appointment, — to call; but a man should keep the most trivial engagements with a woman, and he never came nor sent me word. I was annoyed. It is not like your son to be rude."

Colonel Beverley bowed gravely; he looked pale. He walked to the window with an anxious air, and looked out. "My dear Lady Ellen," he said, as if it cost him an effort, "do not judge Jack harshly. He really means well, but I cannot tell you how sometimes he distresses me. As for his rudeness to you, that I am quite sure was unintentional. He received letters which threatened his peace of mind, and he went away; his engagement even with you — and I know he admires you excessively" (Eileen's lip curled) — "forgotten for the time being. It may be that he left a note, which his bearer, who was dismissed that night, forgot to deliver. I cannot believe even Jack to be so careless, and then he has had plenty of time since to write."

"It is of no consequence," said Eileen, in her heart very angry with Jack. To decide not to keep the appointment — to flee from her — was one thing; to forget all about her was another! She had seldom been forgotten, — this sovereign lady!

A man who gazes into your eyes with all the ardor he is capable of putting into his, and asks you in a heartfelt manner to receive him at the earliest possible moment next morning, must not be permitted, for the sake of example, to ignore you from that moment with impunity. There are certain duties one owes one's sex.

"I do not think he meant to be rude, and I forgive him, especially as there is so little to forgive," she said, with a jerky laugh.   This was her compromise.

"You are too good," replied the Colonel, dryly. "He is not worth your clemency."

"I am going into Calcutta to-night," said Eileen, rising suddenly, "with the Gillespies, and I must really go and talk to all these people."

The Colonel drew aside the purdah for her and bowed.   "I'm going in too," he said.   "I shall see you at home to-night?"

Eileen grew crimson.   "No," she said hastily; "don't come to-night."

Another day of this would be too much for her. Heaven!   If he should go to see Philippa and tell her she had come into Calcutta!   Ah, well, Philippa's gates would be closed to visitors that night anyway, so nobody would know whether she was there or not.

Colonel Beverley seemed ruffled after his interview with Eileen.   That interview had not been what he had intended.   The conversation had taken a turn for which he had not been prepared.

CHAPTER XII.

JACK BEVERLEY, when he went home that night, after seeing Eileen in the Row and lending his horse to his father, was not quite happy. Eileen's manner had been cold to him, as we know, for the first time in their short but full acquaintance. He knew her well he felt, thoroughly; and uncertainty, except of a surface sort, was one of the last of her attributes. She had always had a frank smile for him every time he had seen her, and their intercourse had been of the simplest and most untrammelled sort.

However, as we also know, he had not really worried, because he felt it such a simple matter to set things straight. Jack's nature was of that limpid, crystalline kind, which knows no guile, and does not admit the possibility of mystery. "If you don't know what people mean, ask 'em," Jack always said ; and that rule had worked to the extent of simplifying and making clear a life absolutely without poke-holes and corners. It is true that some persons, not recognizing the possibility of perfect guilelessness in this world of ours, probably thought he was insincere. A perfectly transparent nature might be incredible to

such.   A character without subtleties has ordinarily
no occupation in a world of subtleties. But this young
man saw dishonesty and shunned it.   He was not
good-looking enough quite to be spoiled by women,
— a circumstance for which he should have been
truly thankful.   He was modest without being shy,
which is, after all, another name for self-conscious.

Colonel Beverley was irritated, on the whole, by
Jack.   The fellow had the audacity to look older
than his years, and at twenty-three had a few gray
hairs on his temples, and was often taken for thirty!
The gray hairs the Colonel resented especially, as a
personal affront to himself.   "The very idea of a
boy turning gray!" he exclaimed.   "I never had
a white hair until I was five-and-forty."   The Colonel was not much over that age now.

The announcement of his orders for India made
Jack very happy.   He had longed always to be with
his father.   They were the only two in the family
now, and Jack had pictured to himself a thousand
times the joys of ministering to "dear old dad;" but
"dear old dad" had no idea of being ministered
unto, and Jack was given to understand that fact
very early in his Indian career.

Colonel Beverley did everything better than Jack.
He rode superbly; was an admirable tiger-hunter
with a great record; was also a renowned slayer of
boars, fencer, tent-pegger, sheep-quarterer, — there
was nothing he could not do.   He was an Adonis
in point of looks too; every unattached woman in
India sighed for him, and some of the attached.
And Jack learned soon that his rôle was that of a

very young son, following, as well as he could, a very long way after, an accomplished parent. Admiring and revering that parent, perfectly contented with his position in regard to him, Jack found no difficulty in leading a happy and jolly life in Calcutta, for he had no vanity. His duties were light; and therein lay Jack's only source of discontent. He was aide-de-camp to the Lieutenant-Governor of Bengal, and that kind of work did not suit him. It was only temporary, however, — this position, — for soon he expected to be detailed on special duty.

A few weeks before our story opened, he had met Lady Eileen Beaufort, who had just arrived in India for the second time. She had come to play tennis at Belvedere, the Lieutenant-Governor's house; then to dinner on the same night, then to a ball. Every day after that saw them together somewhere. Opportunities were frequent; and when they did not come of themselves, they were easily brought about by the smitten Captain, who at the end of a very few days was in love to his finger-tips and the roots of his hair. His love was violent; yet finding no opposition, he was not unhappy. On the contrary, he grew sunnier and more genial; pensive at times, of course, but smiling, as a rule, broadly on all the world. His was no cankering passion to gloom and grow morbid over. It was so patent that all the world might see; and if she had refused him, Jack would not have minded the world's seeing his misery, either.

He had asked Eileen on the Row if he might see her the next day. He must tell her — tell her?

he had already told her in a hundred ways — he must tell her with his lips that he loved her with all his heart, and that he hoped to make her his wife, bold as the hope might seem.

Colonel Beverley was standing in the doorway when Jack came home to dress for dinner. The Lieutenant-Governor had been away on an unofficial tour, and Jack was living with his father at his father's house on Outram Street.

"There 's a despatch for you," said the Colonel.

Jack strode in, tossed his whip to the bearer, and stood by the table reading it. His face clouded, " I say, father," he called out, " I 'm sent for to go to Dinapore to-night. It 's a beastly bore. How can I do it with two or three engagements on hand?"

The Colonel shrugged his shoulders. " Social engagements have to fly when duty calls," he laughed. " It may be about your appointment. You ought really to go. What 's up that you can't?"

" Nothing," said Jack, trembling, — " nothing, really. My own selfish pleasure, that 's all; that can wait. I must go at ten. But, oh, father," he called out again, " I must tell you — sit down a minute," for the Colonel was looking at his watch uneasily and turning toward the door. " I know you have to dress. I won't keep you a minute. Father, you know how I feel about Lady Eileen Beaufort. You have seen us together. You approve of it; why should you not? I was going to see her to-morrow to settle the matter. I will write to her to-night instead. You will look after her a little,

father? Tell her I shall be back soon, — that I
have no other thought — "

"Jack," said his father, laughing, "you are maud-
lin. For Heaven's sake, don't slop over like that
to anybody but me. It takes a father's affection to
stand it. Write your letter and send it. I shall not
say a word to Lady Eileen, nor anybody, until you
come back. It would be indelicate in me. You do
not know yet that she cares for you; you are letting
your conceit carry you a little too far."

Jack's eyes gleamed; he knew. His father's
shots glanced off him; he was sure of her. "All
right, then, dad," he said merrily. " I shall be back
in a few days, perhaps to-morrow. You need n't stop
any longer. I know you have a dinner on to-night.
I will send my bearer with the letter to Lady Eileen,
and she will understand and wait. Good-night, old
chap! take care of yourself." And Jack's honest
face shone with filial love.

Colonel Beverley went to his dressing-room. He
had no engagement out; but he dressed and went to
the Club, and dined by himself. When he came
back, it was early, and Jack had not gone. The
Colonel must have bolted his dinner, for he sat always an hour, even when he was alone. Colonel
Beverley did not see his son again, however; he
stole quietly up the veranda ladder, — the servants'
way, — and entered his dressing-room.

Jack had dined hastily, and busied himself even
during dinner by scribbling on a few pieces of paper.
A letter of the kind he intended sending would
really have required two or three whole days. He

was not a ready penman; but he made up his mind
that nature, not art, must be his guide, and that he
would write what came uppermost, without regard
to rhetoric.   The result of his struggles would not
have reflected immense credit upon the average
school-boy; but Eileen would know what he meant,
— there was no doubt of that.

Kali Dass, the bearer, was then charged, by all
that was good and all that was bad, to deliver that
note that night.   "You are to go directly from the sta-
tion, after leaving me, to Winterford Sahib's house."
These directions were, of course, delivered in Hindustani, or the jargon which passes for that stately
tongue among the English residents of Calcutta.
"You are not to loiter on the way, to speak to one
of your Ooriah friends, do you hear?   You are to
go straight to WINTERFORD Sahib's house, and deliver this note into the hand of a chuprassi, — do you
hear?"   The bearer, who had been salaaming in-
dustriously, took the note and put it carefully in his
breast.   "Take the peon-book and get a receipt
for it in the Memsahib's own handwriting."   More
salaams.

After Jack had steamed away in the train from
Howrah, Colonel Beverley, who had followed him
out of the house and seen him off at a distance, told
the bearer that he was going to the Winterfords'
house himself, and that he would take the Captain's
note.   Kali Dass positively hesitated; his orders had
been so strict.   But, of course, the Colonel Sahib
was equivalent to his own Sahib; so he gave up the
charge, and thought no more about it.   That night

the letter was reduced to ashes by the fond father; and the next morning Kali Dass, on some trifling pretext, was dismissed. He made himself so troublesome by his outcries, however, that a place was found for him out of town and he disappeared quietly at last.

The next thing was to keep Jack away; for it is unnecessary now to state that Colonel Beverley's rôle was anything but that of a devoted father-in-law, and that he had decided prospects in the matrimonial line for himself, — prospects with which Jack materially interfered.

He had been cool and crafty. It would not have done to say one word against Eileen to Jack, of course, nor much against Jack to Eileen. The only thing to be done was what he had done, — to poison Eileen's mind a little against Jack, and to remove Jack and to muzzle him for a time until he could press his own suit. He knew well that the moment for his own declaration had not come; he did not dare hurry it, nor did he dare let his real feeling show for an instant. Eileen had still a soft spot in her heart for Jack, and she might suspect if he overdid by one jot his interest in her. It galled him horribly that Jack should have made the impression he himself had aspired to make. The Colonel's vanity formed a large share of him. He was vain of his looks and of his fascinations; and here was Jack, ugly, awkward, untrained, winning the smiles, at any rate, and the approval of the sweetest creature in Calcutta, while he could not boast of anything so far but a kind of girlish admiration which turned his very soul sick, because it made him feel that he was looked upon as elderly. Now, however, he could devote himself to the task in hand; and to say truth, he had made good strides up to the Sunday at Barrackpore.

Colonel Denham-Browne at Dinapore was an intimate friend of Colonel Beverley's, and was under great obligation to him on account of some pecuniary affair in which the Colonel had obliged him. Colonel Beverley had been so eager to get Jack off at once that he had written Colonel Denham-Browne to send for Jack by telegraph. "I want you to see him and find out what stuff he is made of," wrote Colonel Beverley; "and keep him a few days, a week, if you can, or longer. Busy him. He's in mischief here, the dog, and I want the thing to blow over. Only a boyish escapade, but awfully annoying to me, you know. If you have an errand up in the remote Northwest, send him there. I will manage that affair of the shekels for you, and be glad. Don't fail me in this, that's all; and above everything, don't let the boy come back, not even 'just to attend to a little business,' for that's the excuse he'll make. He's headstrong, and will cook his goose in fifteen minutes, if he comes back here. I shall be more grateful than I can ever tell."

CHAPTER XIII.

MR. WARWICK, in Calcutta colloquial, "lived over his office;" that is to say, he dwelt in luxurious bachelor-apartments on the first floor of the great banking-house of Millanders, Farquharson, & Co., the most important of all the English firms in Calcutta at that time. Mr. Warwick, being the senior partner of the firm and the only bachelor in the establishment, lived alone, or nominally so. He usually had two or three young fellows stopping with him, and often whole parties of travellers.

Just now he was entertaining a Mr. and Mrs. Maynard from America, — "New York or Chicago or somewhere," as Lady Barney Winterford would have said.

Mr. Maynard was a constituent of the great firm, and his orders were so massive as to entitle him to respect. In addition to that recommendation he had a charming wife. Mr. Warwick, on his way back from England the last time, had been on the same steamer with the Maynards, and had become intimate with them, — perhaps more so with the wife than with the husband. Mr. Maynard was a little loud-talking, a little "fussy," and a little pompous, and Mr. Warwick was almost silent. Mr. Maynard

was going round the world in search of " pointers,"
as he called them, and was collecting them at the
rate of a dozen a minute. Nothing escaped him;
he was watching incessantly, listening, poking, peer-
ing here, there, and everywhere. To Mrs. Maynard,
who was as exquisitely refined as the traditional
duchess is supposed to be and is not, he must have
been at times mortifying. But she bore him in
every phase without a flinch. His deference to her
was almost courtly; and the ground upon which she
trod, he had the air of adoring.

Mrs. Maynard had been twice married, and had a
history. There were faint lines of suffering in her
face, upon which a kind of heroic peace had settled;
but her smile was brilliant still, and her manner told
of anything but weariness of spirit. She was cheerful, handsome, dignified, and utterly un-American,
as Mr. Warwick, who did not know, conceived that
adjective. He had talked with her by the hour,
found her deeply read, intelligent even to learning,
and possessed of conversational powers which dazzled the sober Englishman.

Eileen had been on this same voyage, and she
had grown intimate with Mrs. Maynard too. It was
by means of this friendship between the two women
that Mr. Warwick had learned first to observe, then
to adore. Eileen was a little bit wild on board,
bewitchingly and picturesquely so, doing unconventional things, flirting a good deal; but there was
hardly a moment when she was not glad to leave
her admirers and sit down by Mrs. Maynard for a
quiet talk. Mr. Warwick usually joined them. At

first he was dazzled by her quickness. She left him out of sight by the rapidity of her speech, motion, and thought. But slowly and steadily he found himself unable to imagine life without her absorbing presence.

Mrs. Maynard did not know Eileen's history perfectly, but she knew enough to feel certain that there must be sad moments in her life now. Of the early marriage Mrs. Maynard had learned that it was disastrous, wretched, damning, — at least it would have been this last, if her husband had lived. Of the effect upon this seemingly airy nature, it was impossible to judge in the very least. The older woman watched for undercurrents of unhappiness, for wistful far-away looks, for any of the traditional signs of hidden sorrows. All were wanting, and Mrs. Maynard came to think in time that Eileen was not acting a part; for if ever sincerity and honesty shone from truthful eyes, they seemed to look out from Eileen Beaufort's. Yet how could it be, thought Mrs. Maynard, that a girl of twenty-one even could have gone through so fearful an experience without a trace of it, without one line, to mark the channel of shot and shell? A girl of twenty-one, who possessed intelligence and sensibility too, — how could such an anomaly exist? And Mrs. Maynard was miserable at the conclusion forced upon her that so beautiful a creature could be so callous.

On the evening of the day that Eileen had dismissed Mr. Warwick, or he had dismissed her, the conversation turned at dinner upon her, to the

9

great discomfiture of the host, Mr. Warwick himself. There were some bankers and their wives who had been asked to meet the Maynards, and Mr. Maynard had, with his usual thirst for information, propounded a great many questions about Calcutta society (having in the daytime mastered the Calcutta methods of doing business). Thanks to Mr. Warwick's position, the Maynards had been asked to various entertainments at Government House, to large parties, and to dinners ; but of a certain set they as yet knew nothing. Eileen had been to see Mrs. Maynard, and had driven her out, and had taken her to call upon Philippa, after the fashion of society at Calcutta, which decrees that new-comers shall pay the first visit. Philippa had punctiliously returned the visit, appearing at her stiffest and most conventional. She had then asked the Maynards to dinner ; but they had left Calcutta then for a tour in the northwest, and when they came back, no more civilities had been exchanged. Mrs. Maynard was disappointed, for she had hoped to know Eileen better and better, and to penetrate beneath the surface or behind the mask. She had made no headway, and as Eileen was always with a party of persons of whom she knew nothing, she really made slight progress.

"You ask me," said Mr. Carruthers-Smythe, one of the guests, "about the sets in Calcutta. I can hardly answer that. Rank here is purely official. When the Prince of Wales was here, the Viceroy outranked him officially. I, as a banker, have the lowest position above a broker. Some of the Viceroy's aides outrank him socially. But they are usually last at a dinner. Our English ideas are really reversed out here."

Mr. Maynard's eyes and ears were very wide open. This was all grist for his mill. How he would talk when he got home ! He was not sure that he could not, with his wife's assistance, — she who had " grammar and spelling for two," — write a book.

" Where do I come in?" he asked with a kind of solemn twinkle.

" I doubt if you come in at all," his wife said, laughing, " except by courtesy. Any visitor, of course, is given a proud position. I am sure we have been treated royally here."

" Oh, there are American merchants living here," said Mr. Carruthers-Smythe. " They hold, I suppose, a position under the English in the same class. How is that, Warwick?"

" I don't know, I am sure," answered that gentleman, who had been given leeway, by the glibness of the conversation, for his own gloomy thoughts. " I remember one night at Belvedere at a dinner an American merchant was standing by me, when the aide whispered him to take a lady — rather a swell — into dinner. ' What !' he exclaimed, ' that woman given to me? There must be a tin-pedler here, if I am exalted like that.' It amused me very much. I fancied that the poor fellow had usually been one of those left-over men at Calcutta dinners, who, it seems to me, are asked simply to be fed."

" But you see there are so many extra men in

India," spoke Mrs. Gedbourne, the wife of another
merchant, " one would never get through one's
visiting-list, unless, indeed, one gave dinners to men
alone, now and then, to catch up." Mrs. Gedbourne
looked as if Indian suns had faded every vestige of
color from her hair, her eyes, her lips, her skin.
She was very pale, and almost a skeleton. She had
been in India twenty-five years; danced even now,
in the hot weather; entertained madly; never
missed a festivity of any kind, and was known as
the Salamander.

Mr. Maynard turned to her. " Do you have to
have everybody on your visiting-list to dinner? " he
asked, amazed.

" Why, yes, naturally," answered Mrs. Gedbourne.
" If a man calls, one writes him down in one's book ;
one's husband calls upon him, and then one asks
him to dinner. After that — I mean, after his din-
ner-visit is paid — one's conscience is easy. One
can drop him or ask him again."

" Well," said Mr. Maynard, " that is hospitality ;
but I should think you would grudge all this entertaining people you don't care anything about."

" It keeps us out in India a little longer, no
doubt," said Mr. Carruthers-Smythe, — " those of
us who are trying to scrape a living and get home."
Mr. Carruthers-Smythe's firm was the richest in
Calcutta, after Mr. Warwick's.

" But how do these other fellows live," asked
Mr. Maynard, — " fellows like Lord Winterford, I
mean."

Everybody laughed.

"Lord Barney Winterford !" ejaculated Mr. Gedbourne, a very stout, bald man ; "oh ! he lives on
the interest of his debts. He's one of our privileged class out here, — privileged, that is, to cheat
every tradesman out of every pice he owes him, and
yet to go on gayly at the very top of the swim.
Those are the fellows who exasperate us honest
men, — he, and Captain Stanhope, and Carbury,
and half those army chaps, — leading a silly, frivolous life of idleness and worse, drawing pay from
the government for no services rendered, and
looked up to as our superiors."

"I don't mind them at all," said Mr. Warwick,
calmly. "It's the same, only far worse, in England.
Nobody here does look up to Barney Winterford
nor Vernon Stanhope. We rate them for what they
are worth. We go to their houses, at least to Lord
Barney's, for his wife's sake."

"And his sister's," added Mr. Maynard. "Lady
Eileen Beaufort is the attraction there, I guess."
And he winked knowingly at the eye which caught
his first.

"Lady Eileen Beaufort is, unfortunately, in the
best set here," Mrs. Gedbourne said. "She is not
a type, believe me, Mrs. Maynard, of that set. Her
sister-in-law, Lady Barney Winterford, is a type ;
and Lady Eileen, being her husband's sister, is received, of course, and in fact is the fashion here in
a way, although she is fast."

Mrs. Maynard had been gradually growing redder
and redder. She was genuinely fond of Eileen herself, and she had long ago guessed Mr. Warwick's

secret. He was very pale, in spite of himself, and hardly had let Mrs. Gedbourne go so far. But Mrs. Maynard put a word in first.

"Lady Barney may be a type," she said, "but Lady Eileen is infinitely more interesting to me. As for her being objectionable, I was on board ship with her, and had a chance of observing her constantly. She was a delight to me. What you call her fastness, I call originality. She is out of her element here."

"She certainly is," broke in Mrs. Carruthers-Smythe, "and I wish she were out of Calcutta for the sake of her example."

Mr. Warwick hastened to the rescue of his friend Mrs. Maynard. He did not wish to see her becoming unpopular, and he knew the virulence of Calcutta women under certain conditions. "Lady Eileen *is* original, not fast," he said. His lips trembled, but he mastered himself with an effort. "But her brother is so wild and untrained that she is credited with all his curious actions. Don't you think there 's something in that?" he asked, almost apologetically, taking in both of the somewhat ruffled champions of virtue, and smiling at the same time encouragingly at Mrs. Maynard.

"Nothing whatever," said Mrs. Gedbourne, decidedly, shutting her thin white lips together with a snap. "She is the worst-behaved young woman I have ever seen in good society. She has actually compromised herself — "

Mr. Warwick's face grew black. "I am old enough to be Lady Eileen's father," he said, in a distinct voice, — there was no tremble on his lips now, — "and if I were not, I could say with propriety that she is the most maligned child in India. I deny your charges, Mrs. Gedbourne, and in this house no one says a word against Lady Eileen Beaufort."

Mrs. Maynard, who was acting hostess, had risen hastily, the port and claret appearing most opportunely at that instant; but she was not in time to prevent an outbreak.

"Will you order the carriage — a ticca — anything?" said Mrs. Gedbourne to her husband, who sat looking like a perfect idiot, as indeed might the best of men under these trying circumstances. "This is most singular conduct," she said, turning to her host, her face having taken on a ghastly pallor really green in its tint, "and needs an explanation."

Mr. Warwick had not the slightest idea how to act. He had been furiously angry with a lady at his own table, and had reproved her openly. Yet she had insulted his dearest friend, his love, his idol. He was indignant, ashamed, and angry still.

Mrs. Maynard stepped across the room, and seized Mrs. Gedbourne's hand. "I am hostess here by courtesy," she said. "May I not persuade you to stay and finish the evening? I am well aware what the general opinion is here of the lady in question, incorrect as I believe it to be. But would you not defend a dear and intimate friend, no matter what the occasion?" She turned and smiled beseechingly at Mr. Warwick, who now came

forward and asked Mrs. Gedbourne civilly not to
go. The green hue deepened, however; and Mrs.
Gedbourne, inplacable, glided from the room, her
husband after her.

A quarrel with the Gedbournes meant much to
Mr. Warwick; but he would have quarrelled with
anybody for Eileen's sake. For weeks he had lived
only for her. She had died to him to-day. Only
as a defender from women's tongues could he ever
exist for her now. Poor darling! She was so rare,
so exquisite! How could he forego the right of
protecting her, of removing her from her odious
brother and his odious associates? He sat down
by Mrs. Maynard after the guests, stiff and awkward from the recollection of Mrs. Gedbourne's
wrath, had departed, and Mrs. Maynard noticed
how haggard and weary he looked. "Perhaps you
know," he gasped, after a pause, looking at his
hands, "that I am a rejected suitor of the lady who
was so foully slandered at my own table. It was a
hard position for me, you see; I am afraid I behaved very ill. This quarrel will be very bad for
her — for Eileen — if the thing gets about."

Mrs. Maynard had suspected the fact concerning
Mr. Warwick long before. "I do not pretend to
understand the girl," she said; "she baffles me at
every turn. I, knowing you as I have the good
fortune to do, wonder at her refusing you. She
may have been startled, surprised into it."

Mr. Warwick shook his head, and a sad smile
flickered for an instant on his lips.

"Well, I repeat, I don't understand her, and I

truly don't know what to say to you. She may be the very person in the world to have made you most wretched."

There was no time to say more, for Mr. Maynard joined them just then.

That night, before Mr. Warwick slept, if he slept at all, he wrote — wrote, do I say? — he dashed off a note to Eileen. He was shaken out of himself; he hardly knew what he did. For the first time in his life he behaved like a madman or a school-boy. "Eileen darling," the steady old banker began, " if you can make up your mind to bear with a clod under your pretty feet, let me be that lump of earth. Let me be your slave. I cannot bear it without you, Eileen. The world is dark without the sun. Come ! You shall live on a golden throne, and be clothed in diamond stuffs. Only be my adored wife ! " There was more, but it grew worse instead of better. And when he had traced these youthful phrases and signed them with his name, had sealed the envelope and written the worshipped object's title thereon, our middle-aged man of business went to bed from sheer exhaustion.

And Eileen, crying as she did so, wrote him that she could never be his wife, only his truest and best and most loving friend forever. Her mood had changed, and to save her very life she could not have said yes to Mr. Warwick's frenzied appeal. Better filthy rags than cloth of diamonds, taking all from a man like that and giving him nothing but respect, which might turn into hatred, if she were tied to him. The sight of his piteous, agonizing love would have chilled her marrow, instead of firing her with a like passion.

Jack Beverley trampling upon her, and she trampling upon Mr. Warwick ! What a criss-cross, muddled-up universe it was ! she thought. Poor Eileen ! and poor Jack ! and poor, poor Mr. Warwick !

CHAPTER XIV.

THE morning Philippa was to start for England came at last. Of course she had not slept; and of course she was much excited, in a tragic way. It was necessary to egg herself on, every moment, with recollections of Barney's disgraceful behavior, in order to keep up her courage at all. Often and often she had been on the point of breaking down, and giving up her project; but usually from timidity only, and not from any failing of her purpose. She was afraid of attempting the voyage alone. A woman whose husband had died in India and who had been left destitute there, was anxious to get back to England, and Philippa had engaged her as her maid for the passage.

Of Barney in a sentimental way Philippa would not think. Barney had treated her like the earth beneath his feet, and the earth beneath his feet had given way; he might well be cast into the depths beneath.

Philippa — a little behind time, she feared — seated herself in the carriage, and gave orders to the coachman to drive to the Ghaut. The servants had been giving her some slight trouble for the last few days, scenting her departure in the air. They had approached her with low salaams, and begged for recommendation. She had assured one and all that the Sahib would be back soon, and that he would look after them. They were not wholly satisfied, and this morning the whole staff was out, — all the bearers and khidmutgars and chuprassis, — even the cook, whom she had never seen, with his scantily clad minions, — the gardeners, grooms, lodge-keeper, washermen, — the large retinue in a body, in short; looking, poor Philippa fancied, as if they meant to be troublesome. It was nearly the end of the month, and their wages were due. She had not money enough in the world to pay them. They might hinder her from going. How foolish, how foolhardy she had been, to attempt this tremendous step without a man to help her! And she had let Eileen go too. There was nobody. She was terri-fied. Several naked grooms were gesticulating rather wildly among themselves. The coachman, one of the most loyal of her retainers, was looking at Lady Barney, only waiting for her signal to lay about him with his whip; and Philippa, almost faint-ing from fright, drew herself up on the seat and spoke boldly and loudly in Hindustani. "I am go-ing away," she said, "on a visit. The Sahib will be back in a few days. If you do not take the best care of everything, you will not be paid one pice for the whole month. Go on!" And the coach-man flourished his whip, and started up his horses. Two of the disaffected grooms seized and held them plunging. Those who were running with this pair, and who were already at the gate, hearing the coachman shout, came dashing to the rescue. A fight now followed; and the poor woman, white to the lips, sat as if petrified. There were only a few disloyal servants among the others, and a faithful Hindu bearer rushed to the carriage to help the frightened creature to alight. The grooms, who had tried to impede her progress, seeing the carriage empty, now sneaked away to the stables. It had been only a scare; none of the others had really joined in. But Philippa was afraid to try to make another attempt.

While she was standing upon the steps, deliberating the most dignified and at the same time severe course to pursue, — for the prestige of being worsted was a fatal one, — a telegraph peon appeared with a despatch for her. Philippa opened it mechanically. It was from Captain Stanhope. "Barney has been badly hurt in foot; we are bringing him home." The revulsion of feeling which shook Philippa was magical. Barney hurt! What if she had gone to England and he had died from neglect, — her neglect! Great Heaven! How near he was to her now, she knew not, but the first thing demanded was action. She ordered the two faithful grooms to ride to the steamer instantly and see that the luggage did not get off. She gave the coachman orders to dismiss the grooms who had barred her progress, and to call in the police if necessary. They were skulking in the shrubberies, and were immediately driven out with blows. So much for example! Then Lady Barney singled out the faithless or lukewarm, and sent them away too, — five or six in number. She looked like an avenging goddess; her face was blazing. Now, to get new servants, a nurse, everything in readiness for the injured man. Eileen would help immensely when she came.

In the midst of the confusion Philippa ran to her bedroom and fell upon her knees. How grateful she was that she had been saved this wild step! She was grateful for the privilege of nursing the scapegrace who had run away from his home, his wife, his responsibilities. No matter; she had very nearly run away from hers, for she saw now, so distinctly that it almost took tangible shape, her duty to this helpless mortal, her husband. There was no mistake about it now. Those who cannot walk alone, must be carried. The children others could look after; no one could take care of the reckless father but herself. This was her lot; and just now, by contrast and revulsion, it seemed a blissful one. She rose and dried her eyes, for she had wept for joy at her deliverance from evil and her power to forgive him who had trespassed against her.

The luggage could not be recovered, the syces reported. The steamer was off when they got there. So Philippa's clothes had gone to England without her; her pet pictures, her books, all her pretty ornaments. The woman who was anxious to go home to England had gone too. Well, that was lucky for her, and she could idle all the voyage.

Philippa did not know the worst yet. She did not know that Eileen was at that very moment sailing away in the " Kaiser-i-Hind."

While Philippa was busying herself putting matters as straight as she could, — and she positively blushed when she realized how bare of woman's comforts she had left the house for Barney, — Colonel Beverley was announced, and followed the announcement himself, pale and wild of eye. Philippa was only too glad to hear his name ; he could be of so great assistance to her. But at the very sight of his face she turned sick and sank into a chair. Barney was dead. She knew it all now. The two gazed at each other in silence.

" Tell me ! " at length gasped Philippa ; " I can bear it."

" Tell *you!* " said the Colonel, in a tone as severe as he dared use to Lady Barney Winterford. " Tell *me !* What does it mean?"

" End my suspense," she cried, " I implore you ! Let me know the worst. Is Barney — "

" I know nothing about Barney," answered the Colonel, his sternness hardly relaxing. But he did not go on, for Lady Barney Winterford had laid her head upon the arm of a chair and had fainted.

Colonel Beverley shouted for ayahs and bearers, who came flying wildly in, losing their heads completely when they saw their mistress white and still. " Pina-ka-pani, juldi ! (Drinking-water, quick !)" called the Colonel. And he himself bore Philippa to the veranda, where he laid her down and fanned her violently. It was some time before she rallied, and he spent the whole morning in the house, afraid to leave her, and unwilling to go away until he had found out what she had been doing.

For it had been Philippa's work, of course, sending the girl off to England to keep her away from

him. Never mind ! He would get leave and would
follow her to the ends of the earth, if necessary.
Nothing should balk him when he chose to accom-
plish an end. When Philippa was better he began
to sound her.

" I have heard nothing of Barney," he said gently.
" Are you specially anxious about him ? "

" Yes," Philippa answered. " Captain Stanhope
has telegraphed that he is hurt. I expect them at
any moment. I wish Eileen would come. I want
her to help me."

Colonel Beverley started, although he dared not
excite her by saying too much. Could it be that
Eileen had sailed for England all alone without a
soul knowing it ? Perhaps she had not gone ? There
was no doubt about that, for several persons who had
been to see the steamer off had seen her ; and Mrs.
Gillespie, at whose house she had stopped over night,
had told him she was going. What could it mean ?

At that moment Mrs. Gillespie herself was announced and was shown up. It was as well to see
everybody this morning. Philippa had her plans laid.

Now that the responsibility was off Colonel Beverley, he was only too relieved that the truth was
about to be told.

" Lady Barney," burst forth Mrs. Gillespie, "you
got the news of Lord Barney in time then? How
lucky ! I have just heard it. But what will that
poor, dear child do when she finds you are not there?
Oh, I forgot you did not know she was going to
England, so as to be with you. We tried every
means in our power — everything but locking her

up — to prevent it, but she would go; and now you are here and she is alone."

Philippa did not faint this time. She staggered to her feet, a little tottering, but perfectly calm. She would not confide in Mrs. Gillespie. " Eileen is a wild madcap," she said, with a nervous laugh. " She has been unhappy and discontented lately, and has run away, naughty girl ! We must telegraph to Colombo or Suez to bring her back, that 's all." Her heart was heavy. It was not so simple a matter, after all, to retrieve a misstep. Roots spread, and branches ramify, and things are out of one's grasp before one knows it, and — for Philippa could not forget the world in her calculations, although a few hours before she had defied it — everybody in Calcutta would know in twelve hours of all the wretched planning and counter-planning of which she, the daughter of an earl, the leader of Calcutta society, had been guilty. " I am so worried about Barney," she said, smiling faintly at Mrs. Gillespie, " that I can hardly grasp the fact of Eileen's disappearance. We shall miss her so ! But she will be back before long, and I have no doubt she thought I was going off secretly too." The mask was ill-adjusted and came near tumbling off, but Lady Barney held it close.

Mrs. Gillespie pretended to fall into the trap. " She did think so, really, silly child ! " she said ; " but as you say, we will have her back and undeceive her. Now, dear Lady Barney, what can I do for you? You are worn out with all this excitement, I can see. I heard of Lord Barney's accident through a man

who said Captain Stanhope was at Mogul Serai when
he sent the message.   Of course, they will be here
to-day then.   Do you want anything done? "

Philippa gave some directions gladly, and the two
guests departed.   Mrs. Gillespie offered Colonel
Beverley a seat in her brougham ; he undertaking to
telegraph Eileen, of course in Philippa's name, to
return by next steamer from Colombo or Suez.   To
make surety sure, he sent a telegram to each place.
And later, one of the Winterford servants sent a
second despatch relative to Lady Barney's luggage,
which Eileen was to bring back with her.   Poor
Philippa did not send that message by Colonel
Beverley !

If she had heard the conversation in Mrs. Gillespie's brougham, however, she would not have felt
her precautions so needful.

" What a wonderful woman it is ! " exclaimed
Mrs. Gillespie to Colonel Beverley, almost before
they had begun to move.   " Lady Eileen was
obliged to tell me the story, and, of course, she
thought it would all be out a few hours later.
Lady Barney Winterford was going home to England without letting a soul know — why, I have
no idea ; and Lady Eileen, who was uneasy and
worried about her, and anxious to lead a ' useful
life ' (little goose !) in England, hid on board,
intending to surprise her sister.   I do not pretend
to know the ins and outs of the affair ; there is, of
course, much more behind ; but it is wonderful how
that woman bore herself, worried and ill as she
was too.   You know, even if Eileen had not told

me, I should have found out Lady Barney's secret;
for we ourselves, when we took Eileen down, happened to see her luggage lying on the pier ! "

" I would n't mention it, if I were you," suggested
Colonel Beverley. " Barney Winterford is a black-
guard, and it was his treatment which drove his wife
to such a step. I know them all well, and Lady
Barney has stood until she can stand no more. He
went off without a word, and left her without a rupee,
I should be willing to wager. I don't like her going
off and leaving that poor girl, though. But I suppose she was desperate, and was afraid of confiding
her secret to anybody. It 's a rare muddle now,
but how lucky Lady Barney did not get off ! It
would have made a horrid scandal."

" Oh, horrid," answered Mrs. Gillespie. " But
I cannot help thinking of that poor thing's simplicity. Why, all her pretty things were taken from the
drawing-room ! There was nothing but chairs and
tables, it seemed to me, — none of the thousand and
one prettinesses that woman has always had about
her. Well," for Colonel Beverley was about to be
dropped at the Club, " do let me know further de-
velopments. It 's a most thrilling episode."

Colonel Beverley dashed up the Club steps and
sent the despatch to Eileen before he had time to
breathe. He then ordered a whiskey and soda to
clear his brain. He was the most determined man
in the Indian army. This girl was not only beautiful
and bewitching, but she was — what inspired him,
more than any other quality, with a mad resolve to
win her at any cost — she was baffling.

CHAPTER XV.

TO say that Eileen was aghast at Philippa's non-appearance is to use a mild expression. She was seriously alarmed, not knowing the cause. But after all, she thought, Barney might have arrived unexpectedly. The idea of hiding in her cabin was a little impracticable, because she had met so many acquaintances face to face, getting on board ; so she put on a bold front, bowed and chatted to everybody, and talked as if she too were seeing friends off.

The scene was a curious one. The Hughli was literally crowded with vessels. Besides the large steamers, of which there must have been dozens, there were all the sailing-vessels, many of them with graceful lines and lofty spars like yachts. Little steam-launches and larger tugs and pilot-boats were lying there or puffing up and down the river, and a P. & O. steamer arrived from England while they were waiting. But the most curious part of the scene was the native element. Here were varieties Eileen had never dreamed of. Some of the native boats are dwellings, like canal-boats, and the inhabitants are more like Africans than the ordinary Indian. Now, one great characteristic of Bengalis

is their fondness for oil in the toilet. They are
rubbed all over with it as babies, and then laid on a
board in the sun to dry and to season ; and they
love it ever after. Their faces shine with it, and it
has a most tidy and glossy effect upon their hair.
These boatmen were innocent of any such unguent.
Their hair was matted with filth. Then there were
hundreds of Hindus on the banks, going to bathe
and to worship. The fat Brahmins sat about to receive offerings, and to bless the worshippers, and to
touch up their faces with a paint-brush. Coming
down one of the ghauts or flights of steps, Eileen saw
a strange procession. Two natives, followed and surrounded by a screaming, howling, surging crowd of
black men, bore in their arms a third, — an old gray-
haired man, emaciated and feeble, in fact dying.

They laid him flat upon· the ground, and then
proceeded to fill his mouth and ears and nose with
mud. The poor moribund started at first, and almost rose to a sitting posture ; but he was too weak,
nor had he the wish to resist. In a few moments
the struggle was over, and he fell back dead. This
was not murder. Oh, no ! This was one of the
sacred rites performed over the dying Hindu. If
he can only depart in the full flavor of holy Ganges
mud, he enters paradise purified and prepared for
the pleasures of his new life.

But now and then there is an obstinate invalid
who refuses to die under this treatment. Perhaps
he has been brought too soon ; perhaps his symptoms
have been mistaken. Mud may agree with him ; it
may have been the one thing needed to call back

the fleeting spirit. At all events, be the reason what
it may, the wretched being lives, and henceforth is
a pariah. His estates are confiscated, and so are
his wives and his children. He is worse than nobody, and his only crime is living. The British Government has reformed nearly all these abuses; and
the many terrible sacrifices of life of which one used
to hear and read so much, — like the burning of
widows, the throwing of infants to crocodiles, and
the horrible immolation under the wheels of Jugger-
naut, — are prohibited under extreme penalties. This
other custom, however, seems to have been allowed
to stand, one hardly knows why.

While Eileen was surveying the scene with mingled
feelings of sadness and loneliness, keeping one eye
carefully upon the gang-plank, so as to be ready to
dodge Philippa, who should touch her on the shoulder but Mrs. Maynard? And behind her was Mr.
Warwick. The Maynards were going to England.
Eileen could not help feeling a mighty sensation of
relief at the thought of Mrs. Maynard's companion-
ship on board, for it really seemed now as if Philippa
were not coming at all.

It was the first time Eileen had seen Mr. Warwick
since she had had that painful interview with him in
Philippa's drawing-room. They both flushed, but
Eileen put out a timid little hand. "Are you going
away, Mrs. Maynard?" she said. "How short a
time it seems since we landed at Bombay! What a
delightful voyage it was!" If Eileen had felt sure
even yet of Philippa's defection, she would have
gone ashore with Mr. Warwick; but she did not dare

count upon it, neither did she dare make an investigation, for fear of being sent back by Philippa.

Mr. Warwick, of course, had no idea she was going. "Come," he said; "we have not a moment to lose." Just that minute he was happy; it was something to hold her hand, and lead her down a precarious plank. She looked lovelier and dearer than ever.

"Good-by," she said to him, with a mixture of sadness and shyness; and then looking up imploringly into his face, she said fervently, "Do your best to forget me. I have done everything ill here. Perhaps I can do good at home."

Mr. Warwick gave Eileen a look of absolute anguish. There was no time for even a syllable. He raised his hat to both ladies, gave Mr. Maynard's hand a parting grasp, and rushed away. Every one of these shocks was greater than the last; and when he fancied himself at the very bottom of the black gulf, still another opening yawned and he sank still farther down. As he fell, rather than stepped, into his carriage, he shut his eyes and everything swam before them. "It has come late in life," he said, "and it is pain such as I have never known." And then, as he thought of this headstrong, wilful child-woman, allowed, because a worthless wretch had once flung upon her his blackened name, to go through the world protectorless, sailing now by herself Heaven knows where, to fall into Heaven knows what new hands, he shuddered. It was keen, horrible torture. He could think of nothing else. He felt himself growing feverish. And to be denied action too! Oh, how could he go on heaping up worthless dust, when millions would cure not one pang of his aching heart ! The only ray of comfort he had was his confidence in Mrs. Maynard to look after Eileen. She would do so for Eileen's sake, for her own, and for his.

CHAPTER XVI.

EILEEN stood on the deck, looking after Mr. Warwick. She had not realized before what she had made him suffer; but the look he gave her had revealed an extent of misery which she had not thought herself capable of causing. She watched him out of sight. He had grown thin, she saw, and worn and ill; different altogether from the man she had first met on shipboard. "Perhaps I am his curse," she said. "How gentle, how tender he has been with me, giving me a soft return for every insult! What a wretch I am not to have married him! It would have made Barney and Philippa and papa happy, and him, — and horrid, good-for-nothing me utterly, hopelessly wretched. I have lost the opportunity of my life."

The steamer got off in time, and still there was no Philippa. Eileen was frantic now. She told her story to Mrs. Maynard, who reassured her by declaring that she must have been mistaken in her surmises. "Lady Barney might have decided to give up housekeeping, to take a journey; but that she intended sailing to-day, I doubt."

"But I saw her going to the steamer office," Eileen urged, "and her initials were down for her

cabin." That did look odd, certainly; and when
the indigent female appeared who was to administer
to Lady Barney Winterford, and whose passage had
been paid in advance by that personage, it was admitted that something must have happened to keep
the lady at home in spite of herself.

"If Barney had forbidden her coming simply, she
would have come just the same," said Eileen; "and
if Barney had coaxed her and prevailed upon her to
stay, they would have sent to the office and cancelled
the order, and they would have told this poor woman
about it," Eileen argued.

Eileen only hoped that Philippa would understand
her conduct, and know that she had not run away
and left her to bear the brunt of Barney or of
solitude.

"The Gillespies will tell that part," laughed Mrs.
Maynard. "You will be understood; but Lady Barney will be horrified, won't she?— It would serve
her right," Mrs. Maynard added mentally. She had
no patience with Lady Barney's proposed desertion
of her sweet young sister.

The lightning current, laden with sand and mud,
bore them by Garden Reach and Diamond Harbor;
the turbid yellow stream became wider, Fort Gloster
with its towers and its hum of machinery was left
behind, together with the villages and rice-fields on
both sides, and they entered the Bay of Bengal. It
was a crowded vessel, and there was very little comfort. Children, and ayahs whose voices were shriller
than the children's, swarmed on the deck and in
the saloons, and made life terrible on board. There

was one family of six returning to England after a long residence in a tea-growing district; and they were like half-a-dozen Rip Van Winkles of assorted sizes, coming back to life, Eileen said. These children had never seen anything but tea and natives and their father and mother, and they were almost stupefied with amazement at the commonest sights. Eileen thought she could have borne it if several more had been stupefied with amazement — or anything, for the noise was terrific. There was a temporary revenge now and then, when winds rose and the ship lurched, and there was great unhappiness among the small fry; but it was noisy misery, and afforded no real respite. The tea-growers aforesaid having had no opportunities of conversing except with coolies for Heaven knows how many years, talked all the time. There was no peace.

Eileen was making the best of her somewhat ridiculous situation, but she was much perplexed. She had meant to devote herself to Philippa, who had done so much for her; but without Philippa she could not go to the old Earl's house in London, except temporarily. She had not the slightest idea where her father was; but Mrs. Maynard eased her mind by joyfully offering her a place with her in London as long as she could possibly stay. So Eileen let the future take care of itself in her old way; and yet she pondered and was serious at times in her new way. There was a change in her. She had, to Mrs. Maynard's joy, taken on a shade of the sadness her face had lacked before. One does not want a woman who has suffered to

look unchastened; it is a duty she owes her friends
and the public to show her grief occasionally, — not
long enough to throw a gloom over society, but a
little, just to stamp her, so that one may read her
record as one runs.   The last few weeks had tem-
pered Eileen's gayety.   She had worried a good
deal over her brother; the affair with Mr. Warwick
was still in her mind, and she had lain awake parts
of nights thinking of Jack Beverley.   A good deal
more sleep she had lost on account of these three
men than her wicked husband had ever cost her.
He had only disturbed her comfort and roused her
anger.

The intimacy between the two women thrown together so strangely for a second time throve, ripened,
and bore fruit.   Mrs. Maynard was cautious and
slow, preferring that Eileen should expand gradually
like a garden flower, rather than be forced like an
exotic.

There was a young clergyman on board the " Kaiser-i-Hind," — an earnest, zealous churchman, who
had been working wonders in India.   Such sermons
as his had seldom been heard there.   His was a
missionary work ; he was a celibate from choice, because marriage would have interfered with his work.
He held services on deck, and Eileen was deeply
stirred, as she fancied, by his touching and inspired
words.   This young man, Edward Mayne by name,
sat opposite Eileen at table.   He had been a class-
mate of Jack Beverley at Rugby, and had seen him
in India.

"The army spoils men," he said, "and society

ruins what there is left; but I doubt if Jack Beverley can be hurt by those influences. He has a heart of gold."

"Gold is hard," said Eileen, laughing. "I don't think any young man is proof against the battering-rams of the army and society. Captain Beverley is like other men, I fancy,— unscrupulous when it pays him to be so, honest when that is the best investment."

"Women have no right to expect much of society men," he said gravely, "because they demand so little; at least, they demand only one thing. The only thing they resent, it seems to me, is neglect. A man may be full of vices, and women shut their eyes to every one, until the weapons are turned against themselves; then they rebel and rail against the sex, which they themselves have refused to improve."

Eileen had no parry for this thrust. "Women don't know much about men," she replied weakly.

"Pardon me," said the other, "they know more than they pretend. You are very young; and yet I have no doubt even you wink at follies in men which should be stamped out like vermin. Pure and beautiful women often do," he said, looking at her solemnly. "I am shocked to hear them, as I do sometimes, gossiping lightly of matters with which they should never soil their lips."

Sometimes Mr. Mayne grew very eloquent, and Eileen and he paced the deck every evening together after dinner; he evidently feeling that he had a noble mission in converting her. He often brought up some flaming argument which silenced her and made her ashamed.

One night Mrs. Maynard spoke to him about Eileen. "You are doing her a great deal of good," she said to him. "She needs to be taught steadfastness. She has fine impulses, but I doubt if in all her life she has stopped to think more than a minute at a time, and she has such wonderful capabilities that I long to see them turned into the right channel."

"I can do such a woman little good," said the clergyman, sadly, "and I sometimes think she is doing me harm. I am only human, and the fascinating way in which she says flippant things is not a very good tonic for me. She is not trained to think, nor does thinking appeal to her as desirable, except for the moment. If I could make her do for others, I should be accomplishing something,—I mean systematically. I know she is kind." For as he spoke, Eileen was seen soothing and petting one or two forlorn little girls whose mothers were ill or flirting.

"She is so remarkable!" sighed Mrs. Maynard, gazing fondly at the girl. "She has too much beauty for her temperament, and a great deal too much charm. Half as much would have done," she laughed. "She is wildly admired all the time, and it keeps her from anything useful."

The clergyman turned again to look at her. Eileen was sitting in a swing, with a child on each knee, swaying very gently, telling the little girls a story, apparently. She was looking down at her charges, smiling and fairly dazzling them with her luminous face. Presently she left them, and came

toward the two who had been discussing her. The
light had entirely faded. "Well done," said Mrs.
Maynard; "you are a good girl."

Eileen hardly spoke to Mr. Mayne. She took a
book from a chair and went and sat by herself, pretending to read. After a few minutes the clergyman strolled away, and then Eileen came back to
Mrs. Maynard. "I've tried introspection," she
said, "and this is what it has done for me. I had
to acknowledge to myself that when I sat with those
children pretending to amuse them, I was thinking
all the time how well I must look doing it, and
wondering if that man noticed me. I also forced
myself to admit that last night and the night before,
when I was talking religion, I was posing too, and
trying to make an impression. Fine creature I am,
well worth your interest! I think I shall tell Mr.
Mayne all about it," she said, hurling the book
down and starting up; "then he will be thoroughly
disgusted with me, and I shall have done real pen-
ance, for I want him to like me."

Mrs. Maynard smiled. "My dear child," she
said, "you are rushing to an extreme now. To tell
Mr. Mayne what you have just said to me would be
to complete the conquest which I fancy has been
already begun. An original penitent like yourself
would be dangerous even to a man like him."

Eileen turned on her heel in disgust, and Mrs.
Maynard did not see her again for some hours.

Late that evening, when they were all sitting
together, Mr. Mayne asked Eileen to walk with him.
She hesitated, but could hardly refuse; so they strolled

off together.   Mr. Maynard saw them sitting in the
moonlight long after.   Eileen's face was in the
shadow, but the young clergyman looked sad and
pale.   He left Eileen at the head of the companion-
way, and came to say good-night to Mrs. Maynard
rather wearily.

"Have you converted the sinner?" she asked;
"you remember our talk of the morning?"

He looked grave.   "I am much interested," he
said, not noticing her question, "in a poor old woman on board, who is going home penniless after
years of life in India.   She has had a little money
raised for her, but that will not hold out more than
a month, and she is too old to work.   I perhaps
can find a place for her in some asylum, but I
doubt if even that is possible."

The young man stayed only a minute and went
away.   That night in his cabin he prayed for Eileen
long and fervently; but he prayed longer and more
fervently for the old woman who was going to England a beggar.

Eileen sought her berth a good deal out of sorts.
She had thought seriously in the morning of making
a confession to the young priest; he had forestalled
her by reading her a long and dismal lecture upon
her shortcomings.   Eileen, like most self-made peni-
tents, objected decidedly to seeing her own weapons turned against herself by the hand of another.
"We have left undone those things we ought to
have done, and we have done those things we ought
not to have done," we repeat fervently and publicly
ourselves; but woe betide the man or woman who

shall an hour later charge us with having deviated by so much as a hair's breadth from the strict line of our duty. "Instead of liking me, he sees through me and hates me," Eileen said almost bitterly. "I overrated my powers. He is shrewder than I. I deserve it, but I don't like it. I am not even sincere when I say I am sorry;" and she recalled a little passage which her aunt had written in her Prayer-book long ago: "Beware that your repentance is not a repentance to be repented of."

She little knew, and it was as well she did not know, that the Rev. Edward Mayne was very busy exorcising an image of dark gray eyes and golden hair, and upbraiding himself for his sin in having allowed that interesting illusion to beguile him for one instant.

11

ONE morning Mrs. Maynard and Eileen were sitting together, — Mrs. Maynard with her work, and Eileen with her drawing, — on deck in a favorite spot of theirs, high on the poop, sheltered from the sun by the double awning with which the whole upper deck was screened, very comfortable indeed, with books beside them, from which how and then one of them would read; soda-water tumblers near at hand, filled with lemonade; Philippa's deserted handwoman flitting about to wait upon them; Mr. Maynard and a few devoted Englishmen running up every few minutes to crack a feeble, time-honored P. & O. joke, — Poor and Old as well as Peninsular and Oriental. It was the time when most of the men were below smoking or playing vingt-et-un, and Mrs. Maynard was telling Eileen a part of her own history.

"Let me guess," Eileen had said, looking eagerly into the other's face, "whether yours has been a bright or a sad life. I guess a sad one," she added, lowering her tone, and lying back in her long chair. "You are too cheerful to have had an altogether pleasant life." It was the first time Eileen had ever employed metaphysics in speaking to Mrs. Maynard; and the fact, with the remark, was duly noted by that lady. "Happiness makes most persons cross in time," said Eileen, "and real trouble either crushes or excites. My sister Philippa has had great worry for years, and it has made her hard externally; at heart she is as soft as a baby. I was wondering — in fact, I have wondered ever since I knew you — what it was that has made you so uniform. I should think it would take years of suffering to do that."

Mrs. Maynard was struck with the girl's powers of observation and of inference. "It has," she said; "that is, if I *am* uniform, as you call it. I have had years of trouble, — all sorts of it, — death, disaster which was worse than death, injustice, poverty. At thirty I had known every kind of woe. I am nearly forty now, and for six years I have been surrounded by affection, tenderly guarded, shielded from the world. But, Eileen," here she put her hand upon Eileen's arm, "the care came too late. At heart I am as hard as a stone; not as regards others, — I am still deeply interested and moved for everybody in pain, — only as regards myself. When I was young and malleable, I was hammered out of shape. I shall never be symmetrical again. Mr. Maynard restored my faith in human nature to some extent; he is the best and sweetest of men, but nothing can restore the original fabric when a heart has been torn to shreds."

Eileen, deeply interested, was leaning on the arm of her chair, her eyes dark with animation.

"Have you been married only six years?" she asked.

"I was married at eighteen," Mrs. Maynard said, trembling, "to a boy three years older than I. We had loved each other, as we supposed, from our cradles; had played together, our parents were intimate, we were considered to have been born for each other. Each of us had a small fortune, so we could be married without waiting for my husband's practice. He was admitted to the bar the day before our marriage. Our devotion to each other was wild, extravagant; one could not live for an instant without the other's society. I was perpetually interrupting his studies at his office; he was always making me a cause of offence to some visitor or relation, by dashing in, and either pretending to consult me on some important errand, or dragging me off to drive or to walk. Of course we were both hideously jealous of shadows. We had three children. After the second child was born, I observed certain changes in my husband. He was preoccupied, absent, often away for hours. I reproached him; he said my exactions wore him out, — mine, when he had absolutely once wept from terror because I was half an hour late to dinner! I accused him at last of preferring some one else. He rushed from the house, moved by what feeling I don't know; I thought then it was guilt. That was our first rupture. They grew more and more frequent, and I degenerated into a tearful invalid. The third child came, and then I took an entirely different stand. Dignity came to my rescue. I affected utter indifference ; was calm, polite, almost gay ; went out, flirted, and in six months he was at my feet again. But I would none of him. My love had entirely vanished ; I felt nothing but loathing for one who without reason had suddenly turned from her who had surrendered her reason, her conscience, with her being, to him. I did not know, then, that mad, selfish, unreasoning love consumes itself in time, and dies of starvation. We led a horrid, frightful life for three years ; an occasional passage-at-arms the only break in an existence of outward indifference. Our positions were reversed ; he was the suitor now, I the flinty one. One day he came home very ill. My heart softened. I nursed him as tenderly as I knew how ; but he died."

Mrs. Maynard, after the first tremble, had gone on in a low monotone, as if she had nerved herself to the task, and could tell anything. Her voice had grown a little hoarse, and her throat seemed dry ; but she pushed away gently the glass which Eileen offered her.

"We had been living on our poor little moneys, and now I had nothing. I said I would rather earn my own living " — Eileen gave a shudder — " than depend upon any one. My father and mother were both dead ; my brothers had their own families. It is quite a common thing in America," Mrs. Maynard explained. " Marriage settlements are almost unknown, and women with children who have lived in luxury always are left penniless, every day. I taught music and drawing, and we somehow existed. I had many kindnesses done me by new friends, and many rudenesses done by old friends, — the usual experience of the *nouveaux pauvres.* I sold my household things; and the very persons who had raved over them in our prosperous days turned them over and over, and belittled them then. Those who had treated me with respect and deference before, now either showered me with rasping advice, or neglected me altogether. I suffered a good deal in my native town, from that sort of thing; but of course that was nothing to the mental agony I underwent, going over the past. What I had done, what I had not done, — oh, to this day I shriek aloud when I am alone, as a sudden memory seizes me and *shakes* me."

"You did *right,*" ejaculated Eileen, indignantly. "You need never fear that you were wrong."

"I did wrong," said Mrs. Maynard. "I made many mistakes in other matters too. I had no really sensible adviser, and I had had no experience. But I have not told you half. My children, one after the other, were taken from me; and, Eileen, I thanked God for rescuing the dear white souls from lives of poverty and its concomitants. *Now* that I am rich in everything else, think how I long and cry and rend my heart for those darling babies!" Mrs. Maynard could not go on; her last words were hardly heard for choking sobs.

"Oh, *don't,* don't!" cried Eileen. "You shall tell me no more; you are a martyr, a heroine. How thankful I am that good, kind Mr. Maynard came to take care of you! How broken you must have been!"

But Mrs. Maynard had hurried away to her cabin. The harrowing recital had been too much for her, and she appeared no more until evening. She had never told her story before.

After Mrs. Maynard had gone, Eileen sat for a moment, thinking, when she was interrupted by Mr. Maynard, who asked for his wife.

"She will be back in a few minutes. Will you play *écarté* with me?" asked Eileen, knowing that he was perhaps not the person of all others his wife just then cared to see.

"You and my wife are great friends," said Mr. Maynard, smiling at Eileen. "She's fonder of you than any woman I have ever seen her with. She hardly ever gets intimate with anybody."

"I am highly flattered," said Eileen, smiling back at him. She was deeply grateful to him just then for having married Mrs. Maynard.

"What a queer medley this is!" exclaimed Mr. Maynard, looking about at the variegated groups. It was growing hot, and the ladies were in muslins and bright ribbons. "It's like a big drawing-room."

"Say rather like a tenement-house at the east end of London. These children, some of them, are cuffed and kicked about by their parents. I have been amusing a whole family myself this morning, who were perfectly overcome at a kind word. That woman over there, who ogles the men so, has come out to marry, and having failed, is making the most of her last chance."

"Do you remember the girl on board the 'Khedive,' who came out to marry a man she'd never

seen?" said Mr. Maynard, laughing. "If we did n't
have sport over her! What do you suppose has
ever become of them, eh?" he asked Eileen.

"Why, we don't even know that the man was
found," said Eileen. "He sent his friend to repre-
sent him, you know, because he was ill, and the young
lady fell into the substitute's arms, and who knows but
that both were suited, without looking farther, and
that the poor fevered youth was left to die? To tell
the truth, a girl who would secure a husband by answering an advertisement would throw him over
in a minute, if she got a better chance, — don't
you think so?"

"I don't know," said Mr. Maynard, shaking his
head. "I wish I could find out what happens in
these cases. I've known one or two at home, in
country towns; but they were elderly people, who
were just mercenary, and one or the other always
got cheated. I got a letter once by mistake," he
went on, "from a woman who thought she was answering an advertisement. She wrote her age, complex-
ion, disposition; said she was affectionately inclined
to the right one, and gave a description of her house,
the room she was sitting in, and all. Some wretch
got her, I suppose, robbed her of every cent, and left
her. It's a shame the law can't protect 'em; but
they make their own ropes to hang themselves with."

"I wish I could go to America," said Eileen,
"not because of the advertisements, but because I
am full of curiosity and interest about it, especially
now that I have known you both."

"There are a good many Americans in England,"

said Mr. Maynard; "that is, they were Americans once, but most of 'em have forgotten it."

"I always imagine," said Eileen, "that all those women who have married Englishmen must have been brought up in England. There is nothing foreign about them, and they take to our ways so easily."

"No," said Mr. Maynard, "I don't know how it is; but there's a large class at home who live only to be thought English. With some of 'em it must be a struggle pretty much all the time. They're always making mistakes. I don't wonder at people's improving themselves; and if they think an English accent is better than their own, and English ways than ours, why, let 'em go over and study 'em, just as they do French and German. But why they should make themselves uncomfortable and ridiculous by pretending they were 'born so,' I don't see. When we were first married, we went abroad, and Mrs. Maynard thought five-o'clock tea was such a pretty meal that she'd introduce it at home. It made a great sensation; and people came out of curiosity, although most of 'em wouldn't spoil their suppers by drinking tea an hour or two before. Now these very people can't remember the time when they didn't have dinner at seven and tea at five, and talk as if they had been born in England."

"I hate shams," said Eileen, forcibly; "but I'm sure there must be some genuine persons in your country. Your wife, for instance, — there is no pretence about her, and couldn't be."

"No, indeed," said Mr. Maynard, decidedly,

"she's as natural as the day she was born. And there are lots of people as natural as she is at home; but the other class is growing and overshadowing the whole country. I dare say it will work off in time. I don't know. We have everything English, but I can't find fault with that always. Our carriages are better than they used to be; we import a good many of 'em from England. We import our coachmen too, and our liveries."

"Liveries?" cried Eileen; "do you have liveries? Then you have distinctions in rank? Surely not."

"Ah, but we do," said Mr. Maynard. "I don't know where we get 'em. I wish you could come over to America and see how very English we are in some of our large cities."

"I would rather come and see how American you are," said Eileen.

Just then came the summons to luncheon, and they went below. That night there was dancing on deck. Eileen, who was usually up to most things in the way of jollity, hid herself for a time; but being discovered, declined absolutely to dance, on the score of a headache. She had been thinking all day of poor Mrs. Maynard. There was a question she longed to ask her, but she dared not renew the subject. Mrs. Maynard possibly had spoken unguardedly, and might be regretting it. It was hard to find opportunities for *tête-à-têtes* on board, but Eileen longed to go to her new friend and hear more. A Mr. Bartruffe, a barrister, insisted upon walking, or at least standing by her. It was a

magnificent night, and they were at the very bow,
looking up at the sky.

"Do you know where Mrs. Maynard is?" asked
Eileen, abruptly, of the young man, who had just
paid her a fulsome compliment. And indeed Eileen
never looked more beautiful. In her light dress,
with a dark blue cloak fastened at the throat and
floating open, her hair a trifle disordered, her eyes
big and dark, her lips slightly parted, she might
have been a Victory such as the old Greeks loved
to place at their prows.

Mr. Bartruffe, who had been days seeking this
opportunity, and who was very comfortable and
happy, answered that he fancied Mrs. Maynard
must be in her cabin. He had not seen her on
deck since dinner.

"As if anybody could stay in those stuffy cabins!"
said Eileen. "Do please go and look for her!"

"You must come with me, then; I can't leave
you here alone," said Mr. Bartruffe, rising as if it
hurt him.

Eileen started. Anything to be rid of this bore!
They found the Maynards on the high deck, in
their accustomed places. Mrs. Maynard smiled,
and made room for Eileen; but Bartruffe was not
to be dismissed like this. He sat down facing them,
feeling aggrieved at Eileen's treatment of him.

"Won't you give me one turn?" asked he, at
last. "This valse is delicious."

"I told you I would not dance," said Eileen,
wearily. "Do go and ask somebody else! There
are quantities of girls on board."

"It's an imposition," laughed Mrs. Maynard, "to keep that poor man at the piano all night."

"Keep him?" ejaculated Eileen; "I would have gone on my knees to him at any time during the past four days to beg him to cease his jangling. He has played incessantly. I wish they would n't put a piano on deck. It's a premium on pounding."

"But fancy a piano below, with the same sort of thing going on," laughed Mr. Bartruffe. "The babies would howl louder than they do now."

"They could n't," answered Mrs. Maynard. "Those in the cabin next me put forth their best efforts at about three in the morning, when even pianos cease from troubling."

"And the holystoning has n't begun," laughed Eileen. "I wish once the donkey-engine, the washing of decks, the piano, and the babies would do it all up together, and let us have a blissful silence. Luckily we all catch naps in the day, or we should be insomniacs. Last night there were some new noises, — invented, I suppose, for fear the shrieks of the infants should have become monotonous and lulled us to slumber. This is the noisiest ship I ever was on."

"We shall be at Colombo soon," said Mr. Bartruffe. "We stay a day there, I fancy, and can go on shore and take a short rest from all this."

"I shall buy tortoise-shell," said Mrs. Maynard. "I understand Ceylon is noted for it."

Eileen suddenly changed the current of talk. "Mrs. Maynard," she said abruptly, "you were reading a tale to me this morning. I forget whether the heroine really lost her love for the man or not; did she? Excuse me," she said to Mr. Bartruffe, "but I have been longing to learn."

"I don't know," answered Mrs. Maynard, in rather a faint voice. "She did despise him, I think, for a time; but when he was ill she thought of what his love had been, and forgot everything but the past. If he had lived, it would never have been the same; they would have drifted back to indifference."

"Was this a novel?" asked Mr. Bartruffe.

"No," said Eileen, "it was not in a book, and it is too long to tell now. I ought not to have introduced it."

After they had all gone below for the night, Mrs. Maynard went to Eileen's cabin. Eileen threw her arms about her neck. "I have thought of nothing but you all day," she said. "Forgive my awful intrusion to-night. I could not rest until I knew. Then, if you ceased to love, you did not suffer so much quite, perhaps?" Eileen asked as if to end her own suspense.

"No; perhaps not," said Mrs. Maynard. "I have never quite known what I felt. It was a strange thing. One cannot criticise those who are gone. I don't know why I told you, dear child, such a horrible story. But you surprised me into it by reading my history so wonderfully in my face. I have no such gift in your case. I read nothing but innocent mirth in yours, and yet I know you have not always been happy."

"Happy?" cried Eileen, looking into her friend's

face with a look of something like horror, — " happy?
I have no story, — nothing but a jumble, a patchwork
of disordered thoughts and unkempt actions. My
one mania has always been to be amused or to
amuse myself; and to tell the truth, I have hardly
ever done it. I am full of animal spirits. I have
to do something all the time, every minute, to
keep myself from bubbling over, like a kettle, and
scalding somebody. I committed a frightful sin in
running away, against everybody's wishes and my
own better judgment, to be married. I hope I have
been the greatest loser by it. As for suffering, I
did not know it as you did. I would not suffer; I
would not think. I loved my youth; I knew that
without it I should command no sympathy, no
admiration. I would not worry. I did not care
so very much. I used to wish something would
come to end my ghastly life. Something came;
but even then I shut my eyes to the worst. I had
been faithful — to the shifting sands, to be sure, but
still faithful. I had been truthful to falsehood. I
never pretended for one instant to like what I
loathed. I did not complain when I knew that at
any moment I might be houseless, roofless. I was
glad when I was free. I was absolved from everything; in fact, nothing need have been demanded
of me from the first. But do not pity me. I did
not suffer; I writhed and winced, and dodged my
misfortunes, that was all, — my punishment, rather.
The greatest grievance I have had for years has
been to bear the name of Beaufort. I don't know
why I was so callous when I was younger, and

should have been more impressionable. So much slighter events make so much deeper marks upon me now."

"You and I have made strange confidences to each other, dear," said Mrs. Maynard. "I used to anticipate our deep intimacy ; but circumstances were against us — me, I mean — for a time. I will tell you why you were callous, as you call it, when you were younger. Your nature was not awakened. The key had not been found. A rude hand tried to force the lock, and failed. With me it has been the reverse. I was stirred in those early days ; I *did* love, passionately, madly. The love of your life is yet to come ; I feel it."

"No, no," said Eileen, blushing ; "I shall not love. I wish I knew what I *am* going to do, all through this long life which yawns before me, big and empty, like a tunnel. I do not care for anything but riding and admiration, that's the truth ; and one of these is laid behind me. Tell me," she cried suddenly, "what *can* I do? There must be something useful even an idiot can turn her hand to. If you could suggest something with a little open air in it, I might stick to it longer."

"Why," said Mrs. Maynard, almost abruptly for her usual gentle manner, — "why can you not marry Mr. Warwick?" The same old question ! Eileen did not change color. "He is a fine creature," Mrs. Maynard said simply.

"Wonderful ! I don't know why I can't. I am rather fastidious about men, and something about him — some trifling thing — turned me a little against him at first, I think. Then I heard my brother and his friends laughing about him, and — oh, I don't know, he grew ridiculous to me, before I knew him. I like him now, I admire him, I do everything but the right thing. I offered once to marry him, but my reason was an insult. He bore my insolence like a lamb too. I hope he will hear the horrid things Calcutta people say of me, even if they are not true. Those may change him, if nothing else will."

"Don't depend upon 'things people can say' changing a man like that," said Mrs. Maynard, with a tender smile. "I am very anxious about him."

"Coming away was the best thing I could do for him," said Eileen, thoughtfully. "I hope he will forget me. I never tried to fascinate him; I did *not*. He never occurred to me as a possible lover."

"No, no, I know that," exclaimed Mrs. Maynard, hastily. "There is nothing to reproach yourself with. If you could n't marry him, you could n't. I only wish, for both your sakes, you could. He is as true as steel — and, oh, so pathetic ! "

"I wish he had n't been pathetic," said Eileen. "One can't marry that kind of pathos. It is manly, I suppose, but one would far rather see a man fly into a fury than be meek through everything. Am I awfully wicked ? " she asked anxiously.

Eileen sat thinking after this talk. She had never felt more discouraged. To have lived a long life of failure, — that was simple enough ; thousands do that, poor wretches ! But to be young, handsome, fascinating; to have been married, widowed, without much suffering ; to be different from young girls, different from wives, different from widows; to be pointed at as careless, even wild, when she meant no harm; and hardest of all not to care at all about anything, — that was her fate. "At forty *I* shall be — what? Perhaps fat, perhaps a spectre; but always a restless, dissatisfied fool !" Eileen was having a serious time with herself.

"Let us talk more about you in the morning," Mrs. Maynard said affectionately, taking the girl's ludicrously forlorn face in both her hands, and stooping to kiss it. Eileen sat on the floor, a dejected heap. "There is plenty of work for you to do, — good, easy work, too, with your powers. You have a wand before which men — and women, too — fall. It needs a little guiding, that magic stick; that 's all."

Eileen gazed wistfully at her new friend. " If I know what you mean, I must have done with that kind of ' work,' " she said sadly. " You have no idea with what loathing I regard all that I have done heretofore. And yet even my resolutions are made in defiance, in desperation. I feel sure I shall hate even your advice, and go my own way, and come to grief. What does it all come to in the end? "

The same old question, asked by despairing men and women every day ! It was the " youngest " thing Eileen had ever said to Mrs. Maynard ; and it betrayed the fact that old and weary as Eileen's phrases often sounded, her youth still claimed her. It was a hopeful outlook for both women, Mrs. Maynard thought. She determined to take Eileen with her to America, if it could be managed. If she were really as poor as she talked, Mrs. Maynard thought she might be made more self-satisfied (in its best sense) by some sort of real work. Her pen-and-ink sketches and caricatures were excellent. She might do something with those. But then Mrs. Maynard reflected that poverty in England — or among the best Irish, which is the same thing — was only comparative. She had heard a man complaining bitterly of extreme poverty, and had discovered that his income was larger than the average well-to-do clerk in America, and that he was only " poor for a peer," as he expressed it. Eileen might have plenty to live on if her ideas could be subdued a little. Then, too, Mrs. Maynard had not counted upon the horror with which her suggestion would be regarded by Eileen's family. Marrying a black-leg was not half the disgrace earning sixpence would be, to a woman ; and Eileen herself might share that popular prejudice. It would be necessary to take soundings at every step, and cautiously. Mrs. Maynard was happier than she had been for months, years, believing that she was going to be busy. Eileen was poor, at any rate, if not financially.

CHAPTER XVIII.

IT was a bright, fresh morning when they reached Colombo. The long jetty stretched far away before them. The green grass and trees looked enticing to the shipworn travellers, for the first week is always the longest at sea. Eileen, as well as the others, was wild to set her foot on shore, and Mr. Maynard had promised her that she should have a horse to ride at once. But a telegram was handed her on board, sent from the Company's office.

It was from Philippa. "Barney hurt, but not dangerously. Come back at once!" and signed "Philippa Winterford."

This, then, was the explanation; but she did not require it now. Barney, poor Barney, hurt, — ribs crushed, perhaps, legs broken, arms, — oh! what could it be? If she could only know! Go back? Of course she must fly back. She rushed to the Maynards, to the captain. The "Bhopal," with her blue Peter flying at the fore, was getting up steam, and would be off for Calcutta in an hour. How lucky!

The Maynards helped her pack her few little cabin things, her boxes and Philippa's were lugged and banged up from the hold, and Eileen, clinging to Mrs. Maynard, at last tore herself away. She had found a treasure in this sympathetic friend, this priceless adviser.   It was hard to lose her, now that she herself was just beginning to improve ; for Eileen had no confidence in her own resolutions, and she knew that the very moment she got back to that odious Calcutta, she should backslide.

CHAPTER XIX.

PHILIPPA had not many hours of suspense ; her anxiety for Barney was almost swallowed up in her new anxiety about Eileen. What must she not be suffering alone on board ship, thinking her perhaps treacherous, at least weak and vacillating? Poor, dear, faithful Eileen ! How many times Philippa saw those pathetic eyes glowing before her ! She admitted now that Eileen had certainly improved of late ; and she, — what had she done? Nothing but repel and chill and at last forsake her. " I did not think Eileen was a finer woman than I," her thoughts said. " I have no very high opinion of myself, but I did think I was her superior. She is infinitely mine." Then a fresh shock and a new sinking at heart overcame her as she pictured Barney horribly injured, dying or dead. How could she see him brought in? She sat and waited. Barney's bedroom was in beautiful order. If he were not bad enough to be in bed long, her own sitting-room should be his. Alas ! it was a desolate spot, this loveliest of boudoirs, now.

In time Colonel Beverley arrived with a telegram. The party must be following it closely. " Barney was bitten in the foot by a pig, it seems," said

Colonel Beverley to her. " The bite did not seem
poisonous at first, but there is a good deal of fever,
and they will have to take him immediately to the
hospital."

Philippa and Colonel Beverley started at once;
and by the time arrangements were made, the poor
sinner arrived. He was haggard, unshaven, drowsy
from opiates, and carried on a stretcher. It was
necessary now to amputate the foot at once, in order
to save his life. Philippa knelt by his side and kissed
his hands, his white forehead, his lips, passionately.
Barney was suffering every instant, and had been for
forty-eight hours, Captain Stanhope said. The first
words he uttered were not altogether satisfying, but
they were words, and that was something. " Stanhope's a brick!" murmured Barney, looking fondly
into his wife's face, then sinking into stupor.

The operation was not performed a moment too
soon. Well, Barney was a cripple now. It was a
choice between cripple and corpse. What a frightful, never-ending time it seemed to Philippa! The
two men, Beverley and Stanhope, hardly left the
place. Philippa felt herself under everlasting obligation to them both. After the first bad days were
over, Barney was taken home, and there he was
nursed and amused and petted to his heart's content. Philippa was almost gay in her relief. Stanhope seemed full of regret and of real affection for
the sick man; and Colonel Beverley made himself
a great deal more agreeable than he felt. He was
biding the time when Eileen should be back, and
he should have his reward.

The first conversation Barney and his wife had was one day in the hospital when Barney was still light-headed from the chloroform and still suffering great pain. He looked always tenderly and gratefully at his wife now, and every look brought a blush to her cheek when she thought of her wickedness. " I can see a halo round your head, Flip," he said ; " you are a saint."

She put her hand over his lips. " Hush, Barney, you don't know me," she replied.

"Where 's Eileen? " he asked abruptly. " Why has n't she been to see me? "

Philippa grew crimson. "She will be here soon, darling," she said. " She is away now."

" Away ! Where? There 's nowhere to go at this time of year. Everybody 's here."

" I am forbidden to talk to you now," said Philippa. " Eileen will be here soon, and I will tell you everything as soon as I can."

Barney shut his eyes. He held Philippa's hand tightly when his eyes were shut. " I don't want to let you go again, and when I can't see you I must feel you," he said.

Philippa was happier than she had ever been in her life. A new day had dawned for her. Barney had been snatched from death, and he was dearer than all the world to her. What she had called worthlessness before was helplessness now. He should never know the loss of his foot, for she would be his staff.

As for Barney, he had not changed as much as Philippa thought. He was somewhat in the condi-

tion of a child who has done a naughty act and been
so injured in the doing that his guilt is lost sight of
in joy at his sparing; so petting takes the place of
punishment. It was very nice and comfortable to
feel that instead of averted looks and haughty words
he got only sweet devotion. He was sorry, and
said so, for his escapade; yet he said that more to
make Philippa happy, than from motives of deep
contrition, for he honestly thought he had been
driven from home by cruelty. And then he had
suffered so too. It was easy to forgive this loving
minister, however, and he felt at peace with all the
world when once his pain had stopped. When that
was on, nothing else troubled him at all.

When he realized what life would be to an ath-
letic, out-of-door man without a foot, — or with one,
rather, — he was not so patient; and there were
days and weeks of irritability yet to come.

It seemed to Philippa and to Colonel Beverley
that Eileen would never get back. One day, after
Barney was settled at home again, she came, looking a little sunburned, a little tired, very anxious.
Philippa flew down the stairs to meet her, and her
first syllable was that of an apology. " Forgive me,
dear sister ! " she said, with tears ; and Eileen hugged
her and kissed her, and smiled radiantly and glori-
ously, and it seemed as if the sun which had struggled through the clouds lately, was shining now
indeed full upon the head of the poor woman, who
for the first time in her life was humbling herself.

Colonel Beverley had met Eileen and brought her
home, and in the carriage, feeling that a moment's

delay might be dangerous and that he had borne enough, he had declared himself to her. He had told her of Barney first, — every scrap of detail she had demanded ; he had told her of Philippa, — how bravely she had borne up and how much happier she seemed ; and then he had told her of himself. It annoyed, confused, and enraged Eileen. It was a horrid time to think of such things, much less to speak of them.

"There are no ' horrid times ' for telling you I love you," said Colonel Beverley, fervently, realizing how ridiculous his words were, even at that moment. " I think of you every instant. I have suffered agony ever since you left me. If you had gone on to England, I should have followed you. You cannot get away from me, from my love. It will always envelop you. I will not say another word to you now. Take time to let me know my fate, but remember my last breath on earth will be the one with which I shall renounce you." He was a magnificent lover ; even Eileen had to admit that. He did not try to touch even her hand. He gazed at her with intense longing at first ; then, as his words grew more serious, his eyes grew more fateful, and he turned away from her. He wore a fixed gaze, then, that was almost appalling.

What a superb enemy he would make ! The old devil stirred in Eileen, and she thought for an instant how interesting, how much more picturesque than marriage, life would be with a man like that, following one about the world with those great eyes transfixing one wherever one went and never losing sight of his aim. A man who could be gloomy over one, — oh, how much finer than the lovesick kind! And in her naughty heart she made comparisons between this man and Mr. Warwick. Where was Mrs. Maynard's heart-broken penitent now?

Colonel Beverley spoke again. "Let us say nothing more about this for a few days," he said; "only, for Heaven's sake, don't shun me! Let me be near you, with you. I am accustomed to do all sorts of things for the Winterfords; so it will be perfectly natural if I do them still."

"Go on doing whatever you like," said Eileen, shutting her eyes. "I am not in the mood nor the state of mind for this. I don't know what to say, and I don't want to say anything. I am surprised and overcome. I did n't know you cared for me, and I do not wish you to care for me. I have come to relieve Philippa, and to nurse my brother, and to make everybody happy, if I can. You will have to be the honorable exception. I can't make you so; that's evident." And Eileen looked languidly out of the window.

"You are a sorceress," said Colonel Beverley, biting his lips. He had with the greatest labor and difficulty, rising early and taking a great many journeys to the post-office, been able to seize three letters addressed to Eileen in Jack's handwriting; but he could not be perfectly sure that in some way she had not got a fourth. Jack might have taken extraordinary means when ordinary methods brought no answer. Still he felt sure that that avenue had been effectually blocked. Could she love any one

else? Would she slip through his fingers now?
By all that was good, she should not, he swore
again.

But he was making a mess of it. He had not
even kept his temper; and then, horrible thought!
it occurred to him that he had not shown the slightest solicitude for her, — open solicitude, that is. He
cared not one rap for anybody's comfort but his
own. What a mistake he had made, though, to let
his selfishness appear! He only hoped it was not
too late to rectify the error.

"You are tired," he said gently, looking at her
with melting eyes. "What a brute I am! A man
in love is a selfish animal, I have always heard.
You must rest to-day, and to-night before dinner
we'll have a gallop. Your horse is looking fitter
than I ever saw him."

Eileen brightened a little; he had touched one
responsive chord. "If I can be spared," she said.
"I hardly know how much work there is in a sick-
room."

"There's no work at all," said Colonel Beverley,
"except amusing Barney. He is in bed still, but
will soon be on a sofa. He has fellows in to sit
with him now."

"He can't drink nor smoke, I suppose?" said
Eileen. "I'm glad of that."

Just then they drove through a flowering gateway
by a salaaming, red-turbaned lodge-keeper; and
there, standing between rows of ebony retainers in
snowy raiment, was Philippa, waiting. Colonel
Beverley, as soon as he had handed Eileen out, ran

up to the invalid, and left the two women to make their greetings.

"Does Barney know all about it?" asked Eileen, anxiously.

"Everything," answered Philippa. "I have told him all. We have both longed for you now to complete our happiness. We are perfectly reconciled, Eileen. I have had such a fright that no matter what Barney does, I shall never find fault again."

"That is all wrong," began Eileen, very moral with the person she had come to benefit. But she was interrupted by the sudden appearance of a bearer. Barney had sent her a salaam, which meant that he could not wait another minute to see her; so Eileen ran up to him quickly. She stopped before the door to enter quietly, and was all ready to whisper softly to him, when she heard a loud voice shouting out. "Don't leave the house, will you, Bev?" the voice called; "stop to luncheon!"

Then Barney turned on his pillow and saw Eileen. "Why, my girl," he cried, "my beautiful, beautiful girl!" and he patted again and again the golden head which had hidden itself on his breast.

It was a strange relief to find Barney so well and so strong apparently. He was convalescing very fast; but, oh, how cross he was! Nobody could wait on him quickly enough; and as for the servants they led curs' lives. Eileen, who had come to her brother's bedside full of stern resolutions, found that her mission was to prevent him from becoming a terrible tyrant. He bemoaned his fate a good deal to Eileen.

"Think of me, an old dot-and-go-one!" he said pathetically. "No more tennis, no more racing, the first fool of a doctor at the hospital told me, and he said I could never ride again. Then I said, 'Give me poison.' But I find I can have a very handsome foot glued on, and hobble round on it respectably."

One day Eileen attempted to preach a little to him. "Philippa is not made of molten brass," she said; "at least her throat is not. She can't read aloud more than four hours at a time."

"She never seems to get tired," said Barney; "why doesn't she say so, if she is? How do I know?"

"Oh, Barney," cried Eileen, out of all patience, "you know she would never say so, if she died reading. And why shouldn't you know? You can't read yourself twenty minutes without getting husky, and you have never allowed her to read to you before. I know she goes away and sprays her throat after one of these recitals, because I have seen her do it."

The little lecture had some effect, but not much. Philippa was only happy ministering to her husband, whom she seemed to feel, with some flaw in her logic, that she had bitterly wronged. They were all going to England as soon as Barney was well. That was settled. Stanhope had paid Barney the money he had borrowed, and remittances had come from England, so they were eased of their cares for a time.

Colonel Beverley was at the Winterfords' every day, — mornings, afternoons, and evenings. He rode with Eileen every day, but kept a respectful silence, as far as his own wishes were concerned; and Eileen felt that in spite of her own will he was becoming a very close friend. Although he was not the man to understand or follow her with the least real sympathy, although his nature was never in touch with hers, determination taught him, an imitation of the keenest sympathy, and Eileen felt him to be at times useful, valuable, and intimate. She asked herself every night if she loved him and the "no" grew fainter and fainter. The defences were weakening; the garrison was on the point of capitulating. The old soldier first stormed with shot and shell, and found the fort bomb-proof. He was now undermining the fortifications.

CHAPTER XX.

JACK had been sent on some mysterious errand to the Northwest. He chafed bitterly against the fate which kept him from Calcutta and Eileen. Not one word, one syllable, had she ever written in response to his passionate declarations of love, and at last his appeal for even an acknowledgment of his letters, if nothing more. He had no means of registering his communications, but he finally wrote to the postmaster in Calcutta. An answer came to him. "Colonel Beverley inquires always for Lady Ellen Beaufort's letters. A great many have been delivered to him, or to his jemadar, Colonel Beverley being an intimate friend of the family. As for the particular letters of which you speak, nothing special has been noted, but a watch will be kept." Then the letters must have been lost before reaching Calcutta. But how about the note he had written to Eileen the night he went away? Why should that have failed too? He wrote again to the post-office, sending at the same time a letter to Eileen. No answer came, except from the postmaster, and containing the tidings that that letter had been delivered into the hands of Colonel Beverley. In the note to Eileen, Jack had asked her to acknowledge by telegraph the receipt of that letter.

For hours and hours Jack Beverley sat in his tent staring at nothing. No son who has not reverenced and idolized a seemingly perfect parent knows how he suffered. The first pangs were the worst; after that he tried to disbelieve. His father knew and approved of his love. The bearer had taken the first letter, which Eileen must have received. It was natural that in their state — his father had written him of Barney's mishap — an intimate friend should get their letters; and yet it was an almost unheard-of thing for a gentleman in Calcutta to go to the post-office himself. But if his father had given the letters to Eileen, why had there been no answer? Even his going away without sending word would hardly disqualify him for receiving common civility. Tom Carbury wrote Jack, at last, of Eileen's departure and return. That ended all Jack's doubt. The consciousness of his father's part in the performance was forced upon him; for when Colonel Beverley was writing him, as he pretended, every scrap of Calcutta gossip, he had omitted to mention the very circumstance in which of all others he knew Jack would take most interest. And, indeed, his father had taken particular pains to write casually of Lady Eileen several times, as if she were there as usual. Did he expect that he, Jack, could be packed off like this to separate him from the object of his passion in a small country, where he could hear from people and find out things for himself? But his wrath was not as strong as his sorrow. His faith in his own father gone, alas ! how could he believe in Eileen or anybody? If a father could prove treacherous, how much more a woman of whom he knew so little ! But in spite of this reasoning, Jack knew that he did trust Eileen.

And now for Calcutta and the truth.

Colonel Beverley had arranged matters so that leave was the most difficult of all things to be obtained, but one day Jack pleaded illness and left for Calcutta; and indeed he was ill without feigning. He was no longer a happy, serene boy; he was a wretched, suffering man. If Eileen loved him now, even if she married him, his life was spoiled forever. Treachery and duplicity in his own family ! He could neither sleep nor eat. He sat staring, starting, as the truth would grow more shapeful suddenly after some inevitable diversion in the course of travel, — a word to the guard, perhaps, or to a fellow-traveller. He arrived in Calcutta haggard, blood-shot. He would not go to the house in Outram Street; he went to Carbury's rooms at Government House. Carbury told him he looked fearfully seedy; so he tried to rest and make himself a trifle more presentable, for he did not wish to frighten Eileen.

Carbury gave him some particulars of the Winterfords. " There 's a mystery somewhere there," he said. " Lady Eileen sailed for England and came back from Colombo."

" When she heard of her brother's accident, I suppose ? " said Jack, dryly. " That 's simple enough."

" Yes," said Carbury, " that does n't sound so odd ; but there were various queer things about it.

However, I'm not a tabby, and I'm not going to gossip."

"Is Lady Eileen as pretty as ever?" said Jack, carelessly.

"Prettier than ever or anything," rejoined Carbury. "She is the only woman I take the faintest interest in out here." He did not like to chafe Jack about his father's attentions to her, for he more than suspected Jack's condition. "Have you seen your governor?" he asked while they were at luncheon.

"Not yet," said Jack. He wondered at himself a little. His indignation had been terrible on the train. With the impetuousness of a boy, he was levelling thunderbolts in anticipation at his father's head. He was growing calmer and more collected every minute; bitter and almost cynical he felt.

He waited nearly all day in Carbury's rooms. It was not like him to delay, but he felt a kind of paralysis of volition. When Carbury went out, he called after him, "Don't mention my being here, Tommy, will you?"

Carbury came back. "Look here, Jack!" he said kindly; "if you're in trouble, let it out to me. I may not be able to help you, but it will be a relief to tell it anyway. Something's happened. Now, out with it!"

Jack had walked to the window and stood with his back to Tom. "I'm going to show myself this afternoon," he said, "and then you can speak."

"I don't want to 'speak,'" laughed Tom, contemptuously. "It isn't that; you can stay here a month if you like, and not a soul shall know it. But

I never saw you in the dumps before, and I want to
help you out. If you can't talk about it, all right.
I did n't know your kind, that 's all. I can't tell
things, either. Good-by, old man; I 'll be back.
Take Sepoy, if you want him, or Caradoc. They 're
both eating their heads off."

"He 's a good fellow," said Jack. "There are
lots of good fellows." Then a sharp pain shot
through him. "And I thought my father the best
of them all — in the world. Oh, how could he do
this, — how could he? If he loved her, why did he
not tell me so? I would have given up, or at any
rate we could have fought fairly. If I could n't draw
one breath without her, I 'd win her like a man or
I 'd go without breath."

The truth must be known, at any rate; he would
be satisfied with that. If there was to be no happiness for him in this world, there was still honor and
perhaps in the distance glory. "I am a soldier,"
he said. "A soldier's happiness is a secondary con-
sideration." Then he thought with scorn of the
time he had wasted. "Tent-life for me henceforth!"
he said. "Fighting, if I can get it; but the life of a
soldier!" And he pitied in his heart just then the
plain citizen who has to bear his pain in a daily
grind of small duties.

It was four o'clock before Jack started from the
house. He dressed carefully, like a man in a dream.
His razors looked too shining for comfort; he felt
dimly what temptations they might prove. Sometimes the thought occurred to him that he would go
away altogether, and not contest the prize with his

own father. Such an unnatural, horrible state of affairs! It was so repugnant to him that if he had not really loved Eileen better than himself or his father, he could not have seen her again, or if he had not felt that his father would be unsuccessful.

Lady Ennen memsahib was in the drawing-room, the bearer said, receiving visitors; and Jack, who had always had the freedom of the house, went up at once. It was Philippa who was in the drawing-room; and through the veranda door, directly behind her, he saw his father and Eileen sitting side by side on a small sofa in the corner. His father was leaning over her; she was looking up into his face laughing. She was in a beautiful yellow gown, embroidered with gold; her face was angelic. He saw everything, — everything but Philippa, who was directly before him holding out her hand. He took in every detail, including the happy look in that other's lovely eyes. He had lost her. A voice recalled him.

"Why, Jack Beverley!" said Philippa, "how delightful! And your father never told us. Eileen, come here quick! Colonel Beverley has planned a surprise for us."

Eileen, rising quickly, came through the French window. Captain Beverley bowed stiffly. His father came rushing out, and with great heartiness shook him by the hand.

"Well, Jack, old boy, you have sprung it on us this time. How are you, child? You look precious seedy. Are you too overcome to speak?"

Jack controlled himself by a mighty effort. Fool

that he had been, he had never counted upon his father's presence here, — his, who was probably never anywhere else. He smiled faintly.

" I 've been a little ill," he said to Lady Barney. " How 's Barney? I was sorry to hear such bad news of him."

Eileen had shaken hands with Jack, in a daze too. She had, not five minutes before, promised to be Colonel Beverley's wife. Jack was faithless, good for nothing. His father was a hero. She was tired of saying no. He was a man to be proud of. As for love, she did not care for it for herself; but she nearly loved him, she thought, and he fairly buried her in his affection. He never wished to leave her side; he anticipated her faintest breath. She was lucky, after all, to be so adored by this superb, soldierly creature.

The sight of Jack shook her a little, — Jack standing before her, mute, reproachful, awkward. This boy a deceiver! It was preposterous to believe it of him. If Jack had been in doubt, if there had been a shadow of a loophole for it, he would have spoken then. He had come for the truth; that was all he wanted, he said, and he had found out the truth. These two would never have been sitting like that if they had not been lovers. He thought he had been prepared for the worst, but he had not been prepared at all.

" Come in and see Barney," said Philippa. " He is so fond of visitors, and he will be rejoiced to see you." Philippa was gay, almost girlish; but Jack hardly noticed her.

Barney kept him a long time, asking him questions, and telling him all their affairs; and when he came out into the drawing-room again, tea was ready, and Eileen gone to dress.

"I'm going for a ride with Lady Ellen. I shall see you at dinner?" asked his father.

"No," answered Jack, averting his face. "I'm stopping at Government House."

"Government House!" echoed Colonel Beverley. "You mean as the guest of the Viceroy? Well, you are a swell."

"I'm with Carbury," said Jack, "and I leave again to-morrow."

"What foolery!" said the Colonel, in a low tone. Philippa was not with them then, but Colonel Beverley was afraid of being overheard. "What is this new dodge of yours? Shunning me because I am successful where you failed?"

Then it was true! Jack grasped the table. His strength came back to him then. "*I failed!*" he said, in a tone of bitter contempt. "May I tell Lady Eileen Beaufort *how I failed?*"

"I will see you later on," said his father. "No heroics here, if you please. Remember where you are, — in a lady's drawing-room."

"My language was perfectly suited to a lady's drawing-room," said Jack, in a low tone. "I have not even raised my voice. You are my father, and to tell the story of your disgrace is to publish mine; but I have too sincere a regard for Lady Eileen to allow her to marry a man who would commit crimes to win her."

" Crimes ! " choked out the Colonel, making his voice still lower. " Hound ! to utter that word to me, when you know I cannot resent it in this house ! If you are not afraid to meet me, as you should be, come to my house and get what you deserve, snivelling cur ! "

" I believe that intercepting letters is a crime," said Jack, " and I have proof which — do not alarm yourself ! — I shall not use, that you have done a great deal of that."

" A liar too," said Colonel Beverley, with a sneer. " My precious offspring ! If you had died at your birth instead of your poor mother, what a blessing it would have been for all of us ! "

Jack's face grew black, his throat swelled ; he rose hastily as Eileen approached.

" We can't ask you to dinner, Captain Beverley," she said with only a half-smile, " because we don't dine any more. Philippa and I have a little table in the veranda just outside Barney's door, and we jump up forty times to wait upon him ; and we have simple, horrid food, because he can't deny himself anything he sees, and rich things are bad for him. Shall we see you to-morrow ? "

" My leave is short," said Jack, not even attempting a smile, but looking her full in the eyes now. " I came to see you," he started to say, but he would not give his father that gratification. " Perhaps I may see you for a moment to-morrow."

Philippa appeared now in her hat. " What ! " she said ; " going ? Oh, pray don't go so soon ! I was going to ask you to drive me in Barney's mail

phaeton. I 've ordered it, and can't go if you don't
drive me."

Jack bowed gravely. The others started, and
Philippa motioned to Jack to sit down again while
she drank her tea.

" Did Eileen give you any? " she said. " Things
are rather irregular in this establishment, but Barney
is improving now, — although he will always be
lame, — and I am so relieved about him. You look
so ill, Jack ! " she said, looking at him earnestly ;
" can't you stay in Calcutta till you are better? "

" I shall never be better, in Calcutta or anywhere else, Lady Barney," said Jack, melting
suddenly under this interest. "I have an incurable
disease." Philippa started. " It is mental, but it
will finish me, I think. I hope so."

Philippa knew that very young men were ready to
consign themselves to the silent tomb on slight
provocation and at short notice, but this she had
never thought to be Jack's sort.

" It 's about Lady Eileen," Jack burst forth, when
they had started and were driving down Chowringhee. The air had revived him ; and Philippa
sitting beside him, looking so kind and gracious and
sweet, made him feel that he had one friend left at
least. " I have loved her for a long time, and almost
told her so, and made an appointment with her, and
had to go away, and wrote letter after letter to her,
and now I come back to find her — to find her — "
He would never speak to a living soul about his
father's treachery. He was out of breath and pale
with passion.

"I used to think Eileen cared for you," said Philippa, slowly. " It is hard to tell about her, but she certainly seemed like it. Lately I think Colonel Beverley is devoted to her. She has been confidential with me of late, and she told me not a fortnight ago that she did not love him and would not marry him. 'Then, Eileen,' I said, 'you must not have him constantly about you.' ' He knows,' she answered me ; ' we understand each other. The moment he speaks one word of love to me, off he goes or off I go, — one of the two !' " Jack's face brightened. "Still, these last few days things have seemed changed. Last night Eileen said, ' That man is simply irresistible ; I feel as if I were struggling against fate.' "

"I ought to have spoken to her the moment I saw her," thought Jack ; "I may be too late." He knew how his father would work during this ride to extort a promise from her, if he had not done so already. His boast of success might be another of his cheats. "I am too simple," said Jack to himself, sadly, "to cope with my father." The drive was helping him however to see, and to shape a course.

"Come to-night," said Lady Barney, "and dine with us in the veranda. I will not tell Eileen you are coming, but you shall see her, and have a distinct understanding. These gropings are horrible. If anything prevents or hinders you, I will talk with Eileen myself. Colonel Beverley, I know, dines somewhere else. Be sure and come !"

"Sure !" said Jack, turning upon Philippa with his

soul in his eyes. " You are a ministering angel,
Lady Barney. I should have died if it had not
been for you."

" I can't promise you much," answered Philippa.
" Eileen may have changed regarding you. I know
she was piqued at your not keeping your appointment with her; and once she told me you had
flirted wildly with other women, including herself."

" I ' flirt ' ! " said Jack. " Not since I knew her,
certainly, if I ever did before ; and I should as soon
think of *deserting* the Venus de Medicis or Helen of
Troy ! She has held me in a perfect spell, — a
glamour. I love to know she is under the same
roof; it makes me quiet and happy."

" There is a great charm about Eileen," said
Philippa, musingly ; " and you 'll find her a great deal
lovelier than ever, unless," she added hastily, for
fear he would not find her at all, " some new change
has come over her. Eileen is of the chameleon
stripe ; she varies from day to day and from minute
to minute. Still, the growth is steady all the same.
Perhaps I am wrong to encourage you," she said
suddenly. " Eileen may be quite the reverse of
interested in you, even; but I think you should
really have one conversation with her for your own
sake, — to clear your doubts and to make your
explanations."

" It will be better," said Jack, " and I am nerved
to give her up now."

They drove a long way out of town. Philippa
wisely thought it might annoy Jack to meet everybody, until matters were settled for him ; so she

suggested the jungle. They talked of Barney; and then his wife, in a strange burst of confidence, told Jack about her determination to go to England, and Eileen's brave decision to go with her, and what had happened since. Philippa, who had never thought much about tact, was more delicate than she knew, in thus confiding in Jack. He had opened his heart to her, and it was a boon to him to find his own frankness reciprocated.

When the drive was ended, and Jack went back to Carbury's room to dress, he felt that he should die unless he could perform some great service for Lady Barney Winterford, who had enlightened him. If Eileen did not love him, he could go away, still comforted and refreshed by one woman's kindness, frankness, and sympathy. He felt now only pity for his father; he knew that a low, one-sided sort of happiness was all he had to expect at best. Eileen did not really care very much for his father. Oh, to take back the bitter words he had spoken to him !

A clatter of hoofs was heard behind him, and glancing over his shoulder Jack saw who was coming up. "Jack," said his father, with a smile, "you owe me satisfaction for a disgraceful attack upon my honor. I waive that. You are my son, and I forgive you. I lay it all to disappointment and bodily suffering, for you seem deucedly ill. I am unfortunately dining out to-night, but I will slip away early and come home. Meet me at ten o'clock there, and we can talk the matter out."

Jack bowed respectfully. " I 'll meet you at

your house, sir," he said. The Colonel rode off. "He waives the satisfaction I owe him, does he?" said Jack, bitterly. " It is much safer for him."

Jack met Stanhope, as he was going in; and while they stood talking, the Viceregal party came in from driving. Jack was no longer incognito, and he rushed forward to assist the ladies with his old warmth of manner. The prospect of a *tête-à-tête* with Eileen acted upon him like champagne; but the thought of the shattered idol, his father, whom he had adored, came before him and soiled and spoiled every vision. That a father should coolly plan to ruin his son's happiness, — that was a small matter, in Jack's estimation, compared with his re-sorting to foul means to do it. If Colonel Beverley had said to Jack, " I love Lady Ellen too, and mean to win her, if I can," Jack would have withdrawn forever, — unless, indeed, he had known his father's case to be hopeless. But stealing letters, lying, cheating, — his own father, his mother's husband, — oh, it was worse than death, a hundred, thousand, million times ! And then to live in enmity —

"Tom," said Jack, abruptly, while they were dressing, "have you ever been deceived in a person you trusted as you did yourself? "

"Lots of times," said Tom. " It's the rule, not the exception, especially with women. If you 're having your first experience of the kind, let me give you some advice. Keep your mouth shut, and lock up your pens and ink. It does n't pay to work yourself up and lose sleep and appetite and get fever, as you 're sure to do in this climate. Nobody

cares for yourself but yourself, you 'll find. I don't
get taken in any more, because I distrust everybody.
I used to call Heaven to witness, and fly about like a
March hare with its head cut off. But that was
when I was young. It 's hard lines, Jack, but it 's
part of the business they call life. Not a paying
concern, you 'll find, my boy ! "

Then Tom had suffered too ; probably not in this
way, however. His was a unique case, Jack still
thought. " I 've expected too much, I dare say,"
he said, " and yet I 've only asked for common
honesty. Any losses such as come in the course of
things I could stand, but to be deliberately cheated
and — "

" Why, bless you, to be deliberately cheated *is* the
course of things, you sweet infant ! " said Carbury.
" You 'll have to get used to it. Learn not to put
yourself into anybody's hands."

" You don't understand and you could n't," answered Jack, quietly. " This thing of mine was like
a thunderstorm out of a clear sky. I had done
nothing to bring it on ; it was no fault of mine."

" Fault, — no ; but you probably confided in
somebody."

Jack started. That was it, after all. If he had
not been a baby and prated to his father of his love,
there would have been no such trouble as this that
he was in now ; and yet it was best, after all, that he
should have known the worst as early as possible.
" You 're right, old man ! " said Jack ; " that 's just
what I did do. I 've learned my lesson."

" ' Experience does it,' " laughed Tom. " There is

a kind of platform of bare boards upon which a man can lead an even life. Without sentiment, to be sure, and with rather a monotonous outlook; but that's where I live. Don't borrow much; lend as little as you can. Tell nothing; leave thoughts of suicide for boys and fools. Jog on with an unmeaning smile. Be as honest as this world will let you, and that's about all you can attain to in this precious sphere."

"You don't make the prospect alluring," said Jack, with a sad smile. "I suppose I am very young and raw even for my age. Somehow I have found things so smooth that I never suspected they could be rough for me. I thought the reason men had so many bothers was because they were not straightforward. I was taught that an honest man might have misfortune, but never disgrace. Now, I find that the reason things were smooth was because I had n't set my heart on anything in particular. I had no wants, so I had no disappointments."

"That's just it," Tom said. "But as for disgrace not coming to honest men, that's the greatest mistake in the world; it's the innocent ones who suffer most. Don't you know those who are perfectly frank and tell everything they know, are always 'done'?"

"Well," Jack said, "I'm going now to dine with the Winterfords. I may be off in the morning before you're up, and I may be about here for a week. If I don't see you again, ta-ta, old fellow, and good luck! I wanted to grumble a bit, and I feel better. We're all in the same boat, after all, and I was a fool to think I was the only one who had got hurt."

"Good-by, Jack Beverley," said Tom. "After all I 've said about distrust, there 's not a fellow I would come to in trouble sooner than that one ; he 's one mass of honor," — this last was a soliloquy, — "and transparent as a piece of glass in his very resolution to be guarded. ' I 'm going to propose to Lady Eileen,' — sweet innocent ! — ' and if she accepts me I shall hang about for a week,' he might just as well have said ; ' if she does not, you won't see me again.' Well, he 's as refreshing as Kinchinjunga in the hot weather, and I wish to Heaven he might stay so ! " And Tom dragged himself off to the dullest of dull dinners at the Olmsteds'. Colonel Beverley was there, and spoke affectionately of Jack.

Lady Barney was in the drawing-room when Jack ran upstairs. " I just a minute ago told Eileen you were coming," she said, as she gave him her hand, " and she declared she had a headache and was going to bed. I have insisted upon her staying up and giving you an interview."

Tom's words about frankness jarred upon Jack's ears then, in recollection. How would it have been to him to-night if Philippa had not been frank? But he felt a great sinking of the heart, for he thought he divined the reason of Eileen's repugnance. If she were his father's promised wife and knew that he was going to make love to her, of course she would try to avoid the interview.

Eileen, in her yellow tea-gown with its golden

flowers, sitting in the pale light of the moon and the yellow light of a high lamp, with her golden hair a little disordered, her cheeks a trifle pale, her eyes somewhat heavy, — Eileen, even distant and pre-occupied, was a sight which electrified Jack into utter and unutterable happiness. Eileen sitting be-side him at the little table; Eileen handing him a spoon, a cruet, anything, — it was rare bliss after all these weeks of cruel separation and suspense. His condition now was almost worse than one of suspense. But simple contact was enough for him to-night. Jack himself was thin and interesting. His cheeks were burning, and his eyes like coals. Barney was in the highest spirits, and Philippa charming, although she felt very nervous about her own responsibility in this matter.

Eileen was positively glum. She did not know in the least what Jack wanted to say to her, — to hurl reproaches at her possibly, as the men who have tri-fled with one are just as apt to do as not, — but an interview with him of any nature would be embar-rassing under the circumstances.

Colonel Beverley, for obvious reasons, wished their engagement made public instantly. It would be the easiest way to silence Jack. He had urged, and begged, and nearly insisted. But Eileen, who was cross and silent all through the ride, told him that she had only given him a half promise, and that if he uttered a syllable on the subject to a living be-ing she would end the whole thing.

Eileen's reason was a sentimental one. Mr. War-wick was very ill, and was to sail for England in a week if the doctors would allow him. He should not have the violent shock of hearing of her engagement to Colonel Beverley before he went. It might kill him, and at any rate it would be cruelty of the worst kind. She had seen him in the morning, but had heard to-night that he was worse, and that was one reason of her depression. Another was that she knew she had made an irretrievable blunder, and that she cared no more for Colonel Beverley than she did for Mr. Warwick. It was her fate to choose the wrong path, to have the wrong likings, to stumble and err and pitch headlong into difficulties always. She tried to be rude to Jack, but the effort was apparent. Jack did not wonder and did not care.

"One used to think blondes should never wear yellow," said Barney, gazing at Eileen fondly ; "yet I never saw you look better, my girl, than you do in that goldy thing you have on to-night."

"It 's old and horrid," said Eileen. "I have a headache, and don't care how I look to-night."

"You 're tired, dear," said Philippa, gently. "Do you know how ill Mr. Warwick is, Captain Beverley? Eileen and I went to see him this morning. We are deeply attached to him, and it was a most exciting visit. We shall not see him again, I am afraid."

"He may be much better," said Eileen, petulantly, "if he can only get away from this climate, which is killing him." Eileen's voice was full of sobs. (A murderess too, probably ; that was all she needed to complete the list of her crimes.)

"I don't wonder you are tired and anxious too,"

said Jack. " Warwick will be a great loss here,
— that is, if he dies.   He 's one of the leading
merchants."

" He 'll leave a pot of money," said Barney ; " I
wonder who 'll get it."

" Oh, don't ! " cried Eileen.   " How can you
administer the poor man's estate before he is even
dangerously ill? "   Eileen had nearly lost her self-
control, and the subject was changed.

" What are you eating? " said Barney, raising his
head from his pillow and trying to examine the
dishes on the table.   " If you 've got marrow-bones
there — "

" Oh, Barney," said Eileen, " when will you learn
not to tease for food which is bad for you? "

" Why, you cross, little naughty thing ! " said
Barney, looking at her in amazement.   " Jack Beverley will tell his father what a mistake he is making.
You did n't know how far gone the governor was,
did you, Jack? "   There was never any peace or
safety with Barney.

" How can you be so coarse ! " said Eileen, indignantly ; then conscious that the guest was badly
treated, she tried to laugh, and very nearly went
into hysterics.   Instead of the lovely, little picturesque dinners they usually had in the veranda, this
was a horrible, wretched one.   Eileen wished it over
a thousand times.   But Jack could have sat there
forever.

When coffee was brought, Jack asked Eileen to
walk with him in the garden.   It was too damp,
Eileen said, and she could not walk in a long gown.

"Shall we sit in the drawing-room, then?" said Jack; "I really must ask you to listen to me for five minutes."

The little sofa in the corner of the veranda had always been a favorite seat of theirs, but both avoided it instinctively now. Eileen, with a resigned air, which would have been provoking to Jack if he had not felt himself proof against annoyance to-night, seated herself in a large armchair and sighed. There was no seat for Jack near her; so he leaned over her.

"Let me begin at the beginning," he said, speaking with great distinctness. "I wrote you a letter the night I was called away. I gave it to my bearer to deliver. [It was pretty hard on even a native servant, Jack thought, to charge him thus unjustly.] In it I told you what I thought you knew before, — that I loved you, and you only, and that I should be back in three days to tell you again with my own lips." He went on without waiting for an answer, although Eileen was now sitting bolt upright and looking at him with gleaming eyes. "The bearer did not deliver it, I know; because if you had received it, you would have answered it and put me out of my misery," he answered gravely. "I was sent, at about two hours' notice, to Afghanistan. I wrote from Dinapore, I wrote from Cabul. I wrote twice, in fact, from Cabul. Not a word in reply have I ever heard from you."

"Why should your letters not have been delivered?" asked Eileen. "You ask me to believe too much."

"I wrote them," said Jack, "and posted them, and they were received in Calcutta."

"Your own father sent for our letters for weeks," said Eileen, scornfully; "you would hardly accuse him of intercepting your letters, I suppose?"

"I accuse no one," said Jack, sadly. "The letters were written and sent. I want to explain to you my apparent rudeness in breaking my appointment with you, without word."

"I accept your apology," said Eileen, wearily; "the thing was of no consequence, and I am bound to believe the word of your father's son."

Jack straightened himself. "Please believe the word of John Beverley," he said, "on its own merits. I have only that with which to vouch for my truth. You do not know that my word has never been broken. I do."

Eileen sat gazing at him with parted lips and bright eyes. She partly believed in him. Alas, it was too late!

"Whether you heard from me or not, my love for you remains."

Eileen started to her feet. "Not another word," she said; "I cannot listen."

"Well, then," cried Jack, hastily, understanding her, "I will not speak of that. Let us confine ourselves to history. Before I left Calcutta that night, I told my father of my love, and asked him to plead for me."

Eileen put her hand upon his arm. "If it is a question of your father's honor, sir," she exclaimed with flashing eyes, "you have come to the wrong person to attack that. I wonder at your lack of delicacy in making such an accusation."

" That was not an accusation," answered Jack, getting hotter and hotter, as he felt himself more and more powerless. " It was a simple fact. I did not say that he had not done so. I simply stated that my father was my confidant."

" Captain Beverley," said Eileen, " you do yourself great wrong, and your father a much less one. I cannot see the faintest object in your visit to-night, or this interview."

" Eileen," said Jack, seizing her hand and trembling, " what shall I do? As there is a heaven above us, I am an honest man. As there is a heaven above us, I love you ; and as there is a heaven, I only ask you to believe me. Will you answer one question? Did you care for me when you seemed to do so? If you did, I will live forever on that blessed recollection. I see I am powerless. I only ask to know the truth. Tell me."

" Answer me one question," said Eileen ; " why did you leave Calcutta so suddenly? "

" Because of a telegram from Dinapore," answered Jack, " from Colonel Denham-Browne. He behaved very oddly when I got there, and treated me as if I were in disgrace about something. He kept advising me not to go back to Calcutta ; in fact, he prevented me from doing so. I was in no trouble at all. I have never been in debt; I had no embarrassments of any kind. I was sent off to Cabul without any opportunities for explanation."

"Did you write your father regularly?" she said.

"Of course." (Colonel Beverley had declared to Eileen that he had never heard from Jack.)

Eileen now interrupted him. "I do not understand it at all," she said. "When you went away, as your father supposed and as I supposed, without a word for me, he tried his best to make excuses for you. He told me how good you were, — that you were only boyish and thoughtless."

It was hard for Jack to hear this. "Eileen," he broke in, "I have loved that man as no man was ever loved by a son. I would have died to vindicate his honor. I have never admitted that he had a fault." Then, stopping suddenly, he said to her in a low voice and with great emotion, "Are you engaged to my father?"

Eileen looked at him and nodded her head slowly. "I am," she said, "partly engaged to him."

"Then, for Heaven's sake, withdraw!" he said. "If it were for his good or yours that you two should marry, I am the last man on earth to wish it otherwise. Leave me out of the question. I will take myself off to-morrow; but I can't, I *can't* see this thing done."

"Why not?" asked Eileen angrily. "You seem to imply some fearful misconduct. Name one act."

"Eileen," broke in Jack, "for weeks I was by you, with you, wherever you went. I read in your eyes that you were willing it should be so, did I not? I don't understand women very well, but

I thought I could not be mistaken. I asked you to grant me an interview. You knew as well as I what that meant. I could not keep the appointment, and I wrote you so. I asked my father to explain to you why I could not come, and to assure you of my love. To do him justice, he did not undertake to do so. I wrote you three times from the northwest, I came as soon as I could to tell you. I have done my very best. Now I will go, only informing you that there are reasons why it would be wrong for you to marry my father."

"Was there ever a woman on the face of this earth who suffered at such disadvantage as I?" exclaimed Eileen. "I cannot listen to your words of affection, — I mean I should not have listened to them. It is dishonorable. I told Colonel Beverley this very day that I would be his wife on certain conditions. He has been, he is, more than kind, more than lover-like. If he has shirked doing for you what you asked him to do, it was because he loved me too. It is a fearful complication. I shall break it all off. I could not stand such a state of affairs or such a life. There would be enmity between you two, and I should have caused it. Henceforth, we will all be strangers. I shall believe nothing ill of either of you."

Jack had accomplished his object in ending the affair with his father, and it mattered little to him how it was done.

In the course of their conversation Eileen and Jack had strolled down and out, and found themselves outside the lodge-gate. The street was quiet like a lane, and they walked on in the cool of the evening. Neither of them took note of anything but this wretched crisis. When they were coming back, a crouching figure, trembling, cowering, rose from the ground, and slouched shrinking beside Captain Beverley, mumbling in a low tone.

"Jao!" called the Captain, pushing the fellow, whom he supposed to be a beggar, aside roughly.

But the man, with great, eager, imploring eyes, clasped his hands together and besought one word. "Protector of the poor, hear me!" he cried. Jack looked at him a second time. It was his own bearer, Kali Dass. "Oh, why does your Honor send his slave away?" cried the poor wretch. "What has his Honor's suppliant done? If he has for one moment forgotten anything, let him be beaten, but let him not be dismissed from the light of his Master's face."

"May I speak to him?" asked Jack, turning to Eileen. "I want to ask him something." Eileen nodded. "Where is the letter I gave you with a thousand directions for this lady?" asked the Captain, in a low tone; for he did not wish Eileen to hear.

"The Colonel Sahib took it from my hand!" exclaimed the bearer, fervently, rushing directly before Eileen. "He said I will give it myself into the hand of the Lady Ennen. Oh, Sahib, I speak truth, I speak only truth."

"If they only ever *did* speak truth!" said Eileen.

But constant dripping wears away a stone, and Eileen began to think that the Colonel had certainly had some objection to her receiving Jack's letters.

"Come to me in the morning," said Jack to the servant, "to the Great Lord Sahib's house, I will see you there." Jack was shaking all over. "I promised to meet my father at ten. It is that now. Let me take you in."

Affairs had taken an unexpected turn for which Jack was unprepared; but he thought Eileen had had excitement enough for one night, and he wished to leave her to be quiet. Perhaps sometime she would see him as he was.

"Good-by to you both," said Eileen, gravely. She walked up to the steps, and gave her hand to him at the door.

"I must say good-night to Lady Barney," he said. He stalked up the stairway, and found her on the veranda by Barney's door. Eileen disappeared into her room. "Good-night, dear Lady Barney," he said; "I shall be off in the morning. Good luck to you, Barney!" he called out cheerily; and in a lower tone, "A heartful of thanks to you, kind friend."

Then he turned to go. Philippa followed him. "It's all wrong, then?" she said anxiously.

"All wrong," said Jack, wiping his forehead. "Wish me a bloody war now. I 've got to fight it off, and the quicker the better."

"Good-by," said Philippa, sadly. "I don't know what Eileen does want, I 'm sure."

CHAPTER XXI.

COLONEL BEVERLEY paced his veranda for an hour before Jack came. He had left his dinner as soon as the guests had risen, and was trying to think what he should say to Jack to keep him quiet. He was not anxious to be regarded in a favorable light particularly, except in so far as that would keep Jack from speaking to Eileen about him.

He was out of sorts. A vainer man never lived; and throughout this singular courtship, in which he had figured as a suppliant, and Eileen as a queen, doling out her favors or withholding them, he had been uncomfortable and out of his element. Women had always flattered and cajoled Colonel Beverley. He was the idol of at least a dozen. Eileen was no match for him. She was not really in society at home, nor more than scantily approved of in Calcutta. Tolerably well born, yes; well, very well born; not rich, not influential, not even dignified, but bewitching, fascinating, alluring. No man could withstand that indescribable charm. Variety was the soul of it. She was never twice alike. He had seen her cross and angelic in five

short seconds. Each mood was more captivating
than the one before it. Indifference became her;
preoccupation, listlessness, industry in fitful gusts,
as it usually swept over her, — everything sat well
upon her dainty shoulders. Her voice was sweet,
her tones were cool and yet exciting. Everybody
listened when Eileen spoke. There was a freshness,
a breeziness which caught the ear instantly. She
seemed less active than she had before that little
voyage to Ceylon, not in the quality of her movements, but in the number of them. Grace was still
the feature of them all. There was never a trace
of real languor about Eileen, although she sometimes feigned it. Even in her fatigues she was keenly
alert.

Colonel Beverley had not really wished to marry
her, until he found that she had never dreamed of
him as a suitor. Then his vanity was touched, his
ambition fired. If only he could shake off the con-
suming passion he felt for her now, he would gladly
give her up. Marriage was a bore, was distasteful
to him. He had been free so long; his nature was
fickle. He wanted a rich wife, if any; at all events,
a distinguished one. But this Irish girl, with her
irresistible allurements, kept him more on the rack
than if he had been the rawest of raw fledglings, and
this his first affair of the heart. To-night his heart
throbbed with the pleasure of his day with Eileen as
if he had been a school-boy. He could afford to be
pleasant and fatherly and forgiving to Jack. Poor
fellow! It was vulgar, this expedient of his. Intercepting letters was only fit for cads. But it made

a simple thing out of what might have been a longer and more complicated task. Of course he was sure to win.

Jack walked in with a dark frown on his face. His father might say what he chose without interruption; he should not speak, except to let him understand that he knew everything. And after the lame explanation — or whatever the pretext of this interview was — had been made, he, the son, would leave his father forever. Eileen was lost to him, too; but a legitimate loss was at least one that could be faced. And he had still her image; the other was broken into a million bits.

Jack's mood was no bitterer than before. He had gained his point in that he had succeeded in preventing this unholy marriage, and the rest he could bear. Still, his state was a trifle dangerous for the tone Colonel Beverley was about to adopt; and a touch of fever, which tent-life had begun, and to which excitement, rage, and despair had lent impetus, was sending the blood through his veins at a more rapid gait than was normal, even to a desperate man.

"Sit down, Jack!" the Colonel said affably. "Have a cheroot, and I will send for a peg for you; then I can explain this little misunderstanding to your satisfaction."

Jack's resolution not to speak flew to the winds. "The only misunderstanding, sir," he said sternly, "is yours now, if you think I am to be put off with baby-talk. When you tell me what you did with the letter you took from my bearer, and the three

letters you took out of the post-office addressed to
Lady Eileen Beaufort, — what you meant by telling
her that I was thoughtless, and had forgotten my appointment with her, together with a variety of other
strange actions of yours in reference to me, it will be
time to talk about sitting down in your house, and
smoking and drinking with you."

" Even the missionaries attach slight importance to
the word of a native, I believe," answered Colonel
Beverley, lying back comfortably in his chair, his arm
behind his head, and puffing at his cigar. " Your
belief in the race does you infinite credit, I'm sure.
You have alluded — and ' alluded ' is a delicate way of
stating your rough language — to 'letters' before, and
I should like to know what you meant. Your bearer
was dismissed for stealing, and has hunted you up,
I suppose, with a cock-and-bull-story of his having
given your letter to me. As for the other effusions,
they probably burned themselves up with sponta-
neous combustion, if they were in your inflammable
style when you left. My jemadar, who is another
artistic liar, took the Winterfords' letters from the
office, and if there were any for Lady Ellen among
them, it was when she was away, possibly, and they
are lying about now somewhere, in which case they
can be found. When you accuse your own father of
stealing your idiot trash, — and I can't put any other
construction on your talk, — you simply show your
tender age. It's time you were a man, and learned
to bear the ordinary reverses of life with some sense.
Trumping up tales against me to make your defeat
look like treachery on my part, is the dodge of an

infant, and does your intelligence small credit, to say
nothing of its insufferable insolence.   You are lying,
and you know it, when you make such an attack
upon an honor which should be as dear to you as
your own."

"Have a care, sir !" retorted Jack, striding forward
a step. "It is the second time to-day you have
given me the lie. Listen to me for a moment !   I
send a letter to Lady Eileen Beaufort, which she
never sees. My bearer says you took it from him.
That alone would be nothing, I admit. I send a letter from Dinapore, and two letters from Cabul, imploring just acknowledgment at last, that's all. She
never gets these.   I write to the post-office here, to
make investigation ; I am assured that all the Winterfords' and Lady Eileen Beaufort's letters have
been put into *your* hands, — not your jemadar's,
but *yours !*   A fourth letter is sent, and you are seen
to take it. Lady Eileen never — "

Colonel Beverley sprang to his feet.   He had been
growing gradually whiter and whiter, and livid spots
appeared upon his face.   "So you set spies upon
me, do you? — spies upon your father in a public way ! The postmaster has been watching me,
eh? and at your instigation? Do you know what
you have done? Do you know that you have been
guilty of the lowest, dirtiest trick a man can be guilty
of? This serves me right," he said, still glaring at
Jack, "for presuming to suppose that birth and
breeding would come out of themselves, and that
a gentleman's son could be trusted alone. Here
you are, grown to manhood, only to develop a set

of traits that would not do credit to the average bootblack ! "

Jack went on, without answering these flings, although he felt himself growing more and more hot. "Added to all this," he went on as calmly as he could, " you wrote me evasive letters, pretending to give me news of Lady Eileen, and giving me less than none, — telling absolute falsehoods about her, — while all the time you were paving the way for your own schemes. I have not set spies upon you ; I wished to know why my letters were kept back. The postmaster knows nothing of the truth, nor will he know. I am not such a fool as to publish my family disgrace. But your explanation, as you call it, goes for nothing in the face of such damning proof as I have."

"And this is what one gets for devotion ! " the Colonel said, with a sneer. " I try to save you from defeat, from being badly hurt at the hands of a woman of the world who was playing with you." Jack clinched his fists. " I thought I would not tell you this before ; but you are so confoundedly hot-headed and go off so at half-cock that one has to be brutal with you. Ellen Beaufort never cared for you ; she was amusing herself. I saw that directly you went away. I suspected it, and sounded her carefully. I tried to tell her why you did not go that morning, although, as I knew you had written her yourself, there was no special need of my interference. 'He is a silly boy,' she said ; 'the appointment was nothing. If he cares for me, he 'd better stay away and forget me.' Of course, with

things in that condition, I did not think best to feed
your flame with bits of detail about Lady Ellen's
movements. I purposely made slight, misleading
allusions to her, or none at all, in my letters to you.
I admit so much. I was thrown with them constantly in this recent trouble of theirs, — with Barney
and all that. They depended upon me and confided
in me, and I grew more intimate than ever with the
family. As for Ellen," — here the Colonel looked
gentler, and in fact he had relaxed from his haughty
anger somewhat as he talked, — " I have grown
deeply attached to her, as her affection for me has become more and more evident. To-day we became
more than friends. Now let *us* be friends, Jack, and
forget all this boyish nonsense of yours. If I choose
to forgive black insults from you, surely you can meet
me half-way, if you *are* sore from defeat. You will
adore Lady Ellen as a young stepmother, and we
shall have great larks together. You could never
have won her for your wife ; it was absurd to dream
of it."

The blood had surged and ebbed and raced and
receded from Jack's forehead, his cheeks, his throat.
His eyeballs burned, his lips grew white as snow.
He grasped the table, to steady himself. His voice
trembled so that he was hardly articulate when he
spoke at last.

" Lady Ellen Beaufort does not intend to marry
you, sir ! " he could not resist saying. " I bring you
this news, although not as a message. She will
communicate with you herself."

Colonel Beverley sprang at his son, and caught

him by the collar. " You whelp ! " he ejaculated between his teeth ; and this time *his* voice shook.

Jack remained passive in his hands. " I shall not strike you, sir," said Jack ; " but perhaps you 'd better keep your hands off me."

" Strike me ? " gasped the other, shaking Jack violently, and throwing him off so abruptly and with such force as to send him against the edge of the doorway, inflicting rather a severe cut upon Jack's head. A fight with his son would put the last touches to Eileen's contemplated rejection, if this were authentic news the boy brought, and he must be well and strong in the morning to begin the bombardment again. He would marry her or die. " I can't fight with you," he said contemptuously. " I have a right to thrash you soundly, and you richly deserve it. But I won't fight with you. Dogs, children, and fools are barred. We 'll meet publicly as friends, although I shall have hard work to keep my hands off you ; one must keep up the decencies of life. But let me hear of your seeing my promised wife, and trying to poison her mind with your infamous lies about me, and I 'll — "

" Two *can* play at infamous lies, but one won't," replied Jack. " I leave you, sir, and I advise you to rap the next rival over the head, or put a bullet through him. You 'll find it a more paying investment than trying to circumvent him with trickery." And Jack left the house.

CHAPTER XXII.

JACK wandered on and on, not knowing or caring where he went. Fever was racing through him; he knew nothing could save him now from a bout of it. "My father gone," he almost mumbled, — "no father any more. Where is the man I have worshipped? There never was such a man; this was in him, or it could n't have come out. And Eileen lost, what have I left? My trade, that's all. I shall petition to join my regiment. Never one peaceful breath will I draw again; and as for Calcutta, to-morrow I will leave it forever."

Jack staggered in at Government House, and found Carbury just going to bed. It was nearly morning. "Come, Tommy!" said Jack, feigning joviality, "let's have a game of pool. Don't go to bed, there's a good fellow! Some of them are up; I heard the balls clicking. Stanhope and Villars are there, I know. Come on!"

"Then you 're not ' off in the morning,' " laughed Tom, deceived for a moment by the manner; "you 're going to ' hang about for a week,' eh? I congratulate you."

"On what?" said Jack, — "on the death and burial of every tie I had, — all I cared for in the world?
I 've just been to all their funerals, and I 'm feeling
jolly, because there is nothing left I can possibly feel
a pang about in future. That 's a good deal to
be thankful for, is n't it? I 'm really to be envied,
now I tell you, Tom ! "

Carbury turned and looked at Jack. He was familiar with this phase of misanthropy too. It usually followed hard upon the other. "I don't want
to celebrate your misfortunes, if you do," he said,
"and I 'm deuced sorry to see you so ill, for that 's
what 's the matter. You 're well on for jungle fever,
old man ! " Tom added anxiously, grasping Jack's
wrist, and feeling his pulse throb wildly, "and you
must go to bed ! "

"Bed?" sneered Jack. "I 'm not going to bed
in this hole. I can't sleep till I get to my own
rough cot in my own little tent, — the bed of a
soldier."

Could it be that he had been drinking? thought
Tom. No, he was excited and very feverish.

"I don't want to see any of your down pillows
and satin counterpanes. What I want is a — " And
here Jack burst into rather an unintelligible strain,
which settled Tom in his determination to get him
off to bed, and send the surgeon to him.

"What on earth can it be?" Tom thought.
"Lady Eileen's refusal would not account for all
this. There 's something wrong with his governor.
There was blood on his shirt-collar too. Oh, I see !
It 's a case of father *versus* son, and of course the

father in this case wins. I 'm awfully sorry. I
wonder if that lovely thing is going to marry that
man. You never can tell what a woman will
do."

Jack could not be kept quiet just then. He came
rambling back into Tom's room, and insisted upon
talking. He was not exactly delirious, only excited; and Tom at last thought it better to let him
go on.

"Tom," he said, "I know you think I 'm an awful baby, but I 've had such hard blows. You
don't know, Tom. Don't think it 's all because of a
woman I am so cut up. It 's worse than that; that 's
simple. Until I get used to it a bit I shall be deuced
eccentric, I know. It drives me perfectly mad. It
settles down and over me like the black cap a man is
hanged in. I can't see straight, — I can't, Tom. I
don't know much," he went on. "A fool could cheat
me. I 've never suspected any one. Soldiering 's all
I 've got solid, and that 's all I want now. Thank
God! I have n't done a dirty action yet. I 've got
clean hands; and if ever I do anything mean, I hope
I shall be drawn through the Hooghli current, at the
tail of a dinghi, with crocodiles biting me at every
step."

"You won't think you 're mean, if you ever get
to be so," said Tom, quietly. "A man falls into it
gradually. What he wants he thinks he deserves;
and if he does n't get it, he thinks it 's others who
are cheating him."

"No," said Jack, "it does n't come gradually.
It 's *in* a man, and comes out. Never mind, Tom!

You're a good fellow; and if I had n't had you here, I should have made a good deal bigger ass of myself."

Of course Jack was not able to go away in the morning, nor for several mornings. Carbury wanted to send for his father, but Jack announced decidedly that that was not to be done.

CHAPTER XXIII.

WHEN Jack Beverley had gone, after that extremely unpleasant evening at the Winterfords', Eileen was as thoroughly unhappy and uncomfortable as she had ever been in her whole life. Although she had been as discreet as she knew how to be with Jack on the subject of his father, nothing but a guilty recollection of the tie she had herself been coaxed into forming that day had kept her from renouncing Colonel Beverley's acquaintance forever, and letting Jack see the real state of her feeling toward him. For Eileen knew, when she saw the young man, so honest, so good, so manly, standing before her, almost tongue-tied, that he was the only being she cared for sufficiently to marry. And he was the very one she could not marry. There was her fate again; self-rushed upon, but no matter! It was fate, just the same, and she could not escape it. Marry the Colonel? *Never!* He had forfeited the right to her esteem ; for if Jack was truthful in even the little he had said or implied, his father was the opposite. He must have intercepted her letters from Jack, and he had deceived her about him. Jack would never have made the statements he had made to her that night, if they had not been true. And all the Colonel's sadness and his apologies for his son's negligence were feigned. It was a relief to know it; for to believe ill of Jack Beverley had been hard for her, whereas she cared so little in her heart for his father. "Oh, Jack, dear Jack," she called aloud, "I could not tell you, darling boy, but I do love you. Perhaps if I could have you, I should *not.* I am so unprincipled; but now that you are lost to me, I cannot live without you!" He wanted truth, she said; and truth he shall have, now that it is too late. And so, after she had framed a startling resolution, which was to take her world by surprise in the morning, she penned Jack a comforting little note, or at least it was comforting to her to write it. The note was laid beside Jack's bedside; and when he could, he read it. But it did not cure his fever, and in fact he was decidedly light-headed after reading it. It was, as the French say, thus conceived: —

MY DEAR JACK [that was good for two degrees of temperature, at least], — Is truth best? And do you really want to know it? Then I will tell you it. I have cared for you more than for any other man. I say "have cared," because, dear Jack, we are the victims of fate, and have been vanquished. Do not try to see me. We cannot trust ourselves yet, and we must not see each other. A shadow is between us, and we can never drive it away. Bear it, Jack, as I shall; and when you hear what I have done, do not despise me. It is for the sake of one who loves me as I do not deserve to be loved, — and who is better than either you or I, or anybody else in the world. By and by we can be friends; not yet, because we cannot trust ourselves.

Yours, ELLEN.

"When you hear what I have done — for the sake of one who loves me better than I deserve — who is better than any one else in the world — " Jack's head swam, and strange lights flickered before his hot eyeballs, as he went over and over the unintelligible words. It was not long before he learned what they meant; but Tom Carbury, seeing the effect of the note, took care he should not learn any startling tidings until he was out of the woods. But all that day he murmured and mumbled, "Who is better than you or I, — who loves me as I do not deserve to be loved," and fell into little troubled naps, still mumbling.

Eileen was busy nearly all night; and Colonel Beverley received one of the fruits of her industry, which sent him into paroxysms of wild rage. It began : —

My dear Colonel Beverley, — I retract the half promise ["Half promise !" he muttered. "Most memories add; hers subtracts"] I made you yesterday. I never should have made it; but having done so, I now assure you that no power on earth shall make me keep it. Consider me absolved, and by no means come to see me at present.

Yours sincerely,   Ellen Beaufort.

A thousand devils ! Jack's work, of course ! He had told her about the letters. The Colonel swore until the air was dark about him, — bright, sunny morning though it was. He had been prepared, and had got up early, determined to open the campaign before Jack could arrive on the spot. The Colonel's bearer had never gone through quite so much at his master's hands — or his lips, rather — as in that morning's dressing. *Jack*, thought the Colonel, *Jack*, the cub, the undutiful, hypocritical, moral son who had worried him more by his candor and virtue than if he had run into debt or scrapes, a thousand times, — Jack has done me this turn. " I should like to kill him," gasped the Colonel. "' She will not marry you !' " he quoted mockingly. "She won't, won't she ? We shall see about that ! I 'll marry her in the teeth of Satan, and I 'll marry her in a month too ; and if we ever have a son, I 'll strangle him the moment he is born."

There was no time to be lost ; he was in the habit of strolling in at the Winterfords' in the mornings. Choking, apoplectic, yet outwardly calm enough, he went out his door and into his brougham. The syce had brought his buggy as usual, and he found he could not drive, his hand shook so. He wanted to carry Ellen off on a pillion, like Lochinvar, while the fools looked on and gaped. Oh for the old days when men fought and won the women they wanted ! That was what Jack had thought too. The point of view changed the aspect somewhat. Colonel Beverley looked upon himself as an injured man. " Love her ! " he said. " I don't know and I don't care whether I love her or not, or whether she loves me or not. She 's beautiful, the minx, and bewitching ; and I 'll tame her, that 's all. She thinks she can play her men as she chooses ; I 'll teach her how to treat this one."

Arrived at the Winterfords', he strolled about, and found no one. They had not breakfasted, the servant said. The brougham was ordered at ten. Colonel Beverley wrote on his card, and sent it to Eileen, "I must see you; I will wait."

The bearer returned. "Lady Ennen was asleep," the ayah said, "and was not to be disturbed." But the Colonel did not go.

After a time Philippa came downstairs. Colonel Beverley asked anxiously if he might not see Eileen. "I feel I have a right now," he said, with a smile half knowing, half tender, and throwing *his* promise of the day before to the winds. Why should he keep it now?

"I advise you not to talk about ' rights,' with her Imperial Highness," laughed Philippa. "Her ayah is on guard, and I was not allowed to put my head inside the dressing-room door even. I received a written request to drive with the lady at ten, and I fancy she breakfasts in her own room, for it is that now."

The brougham could hardly be brought to Eileen's bedroom-door, but Eileen was determined not to be waylaid by her indignant lover. The bathrooms had staircases leading down from them outside, — spiral ways enclosed in a kind of turret. She ran down the spiral stair, and got into the carriage, for which she beckoned. Then she sent a salaam to Lady Barney, who was waiting at the door. Colonel Beverley went with Philippa, to put her in at the tower-door. He was as resolute as Eileen. "Ellen," he said in an authoritative tone, "I am waiting to speak to you. Will you grant me five minutes now?"

"I am going on an important errand now,"

she said; "I will give you an interview at twelve
o'clock."

Colonel Beverley put his hand on the carriage-
door. "Forgive me for being so persistent," he
urged, in a peremptory tone which belied his gentle
phrase; "two minutes will do, but they must be
these." He felt sure she was on her way to meet
Jack, and he must talk to her before that, or all was
ended.

Eileen drew herself up haughtily. "Is a woman
at the mercy of a man, then," she asked, "that she
may not choose her own times? At twelve o'clock
you may see me, Colonel Beverley, and not an instant
before."

The enraged Colonel bit his lip, raised his hat,
shut the door which he had opened for Philippa,
and they were gone. "Damn her!" he muttered.
"She has beaten. She will come back engaged to
Jack, and together they will defy me. Engaged to
him! No money, not a pice, either of them, and
no prospect of any. Fools! She *shall* be publicly
engaged to me, I swear; and if that is the most
I can do, I will publicly throw her over, by Jove!
I have a thousand minds to go to the Club now
and proclaim our engagement. Perhaps I'd better
wait until after twelve. This errand of life and death
may be an appointment with the dressmaker. Curse
her! What frightful airs she gives herself! And
what an exquisite hussy it is too!"

"What is all this?" asked Philippa, anxiously, when
they were outside the gate. "Why do you treat
Colonel Beverley so, and where are we going?"

Philippa did not repose that blind confidence in her
pilot which enabled her to approve, uninformed, of
the purpose of the expedition. She had supposed
it to be a shopping-tour. In fact, when Colonel
Beverley had asked what order to give the coachman, as he shut the brougham-door, Eileen had
given him the name of an English shop in the town.
But that did not quite satisfy Philippa now.

"Philippa," Eileen said, clasping her sister's hand
and drawing close to her, "I am going to that dear
man who loves me so, and whom I have almost
brought to death by my wickedness. I am going to
give myself to him; please God, I can bring him
back to health, and at least I know I can make him
happy."

Philippa's eyes were nearly out of her head. Her
brain reeled at the suddenness of the girl's gyrations.
"Eileen!" she exclaimed, "you shall not do this
insane thing! Why should you? What has brought
you to it? Not our affairs, Eileen? You know we
do not need you to do it for us; and as for yourself,
you know you are always to share with us. Besides,
Eileen, you must stop these wild, madcap actions of
yours. I will not lend my countenance to them.
What have you done to Colonel Beverley? Yesterday you two were like lovers, and you must have
given him definite encouragement, for he said he
had a right to see you this morning."

"A *right* to see me, has he?" broke in Eileen,
her face crimson. "Philippa, he did have a right.
I can't tell you how he has forfeited the right, or the
right to a decent woman's esteem; but he knows

perfectly. I made him a promise, — you know how he has pursued me, — and I was so tired of this everlasting restlessness, I wanted an anchorage ; but that is over. As for Mr. Warwick's money, I shall not *touch* it ; it has nothing to do with the question. I wish he were as poor as Job, that I might work for him. I hate Colonel Beverley," she went on, with a ring of rage in her voice which would not have pleased the Colonel, nor encouraged him, "and I cannot marry Jack."

"Why not?" asked Philippa, quickly. "He is devoted to you too, and such a fine fellow, near your age, and I know you like him."

"It's not a question of liking, either," answered Eileen, firmly, shutting her eyes. "Marriage with him is not to be thought of. To marry Mr. Warwick is my intention. This is not an impulse, Philippa ; you will see. If I am ever to do anything for a human being, this is my opportunity. It is no use to try to cross me now, Philippa. I shall go alone if you don't go with me, for I am determined."

Philippa shook her head, and a very anxious frown was on her forehead. She hardly knew what to do ; but it was very evident that Eileen would do exactly as she chose. There was no restraining her now any more than there ever had been. The coachman's order was changed ; and when they arrived at Mr. Warwick's house, Eileen marched up the steps with a proud, firm tread, while the stately Philippa, mortally ashamed of herself and Eileen and the whole affair, walked guiltily behind with a very red face. In her heart she had always wished Eileen to marry the rich banker, for she knew what a "steadier" wealth would be to her; and of course forswearing it was nonsense. At the same time this was not legitimate, this extraordinary morning visit to a man in his sick-room, as a preliminary to matrimony. It was an indecent escapade, Philippa said to herself; and being a party to it was abhorrent to her. But letting Eileen go through her absurd scene alone would be worse; so she allowed herself to be drawn in.

Philippa could not bear, either, to see a young girl sacrificed to an invalid. Mr. Warwick was hopelessly ill, they had been told, but he might live on and on for months or years. However, there was no more use in trying to stop the young woman now, than in requesting the breezes of heaven not to blow; so she followed in the girl's wake, with downcast eyes.

Mr. Warwick had had a bad night, the English nurse, whom they summoned, said, but perhaps they might see him for a moment only. He was very weak, but the doctor did not find that the ladies' visit of the day before had done him harm.

"Could I see him for a minute alone?" asked Eileen, boldly.

Philippa blushed more scarlet than ever. "I will go with you," she said reproachfully to the girl.

So they went into Mr. Warwick's room; and there they found him, oh, so pale and weak, but brightened at the thought of seeing them. Perhaps he was buoying himself up with a ray of false hope again, foolish man that he was! Nothing but death, it seemed, could extinguish the spark which glowed whenever he saw Eileen.

Eileen went to the bedside, and took one of the thin hands in both her own. " You are going to be well soon," she said, smiling. " I am to make you so. Listen, dear ! " Her lips quivered a little as she uttered the last word, and Mr. Warwick flushed painfully.

Philippa sauntered into the dressing-room, and entered into a low dialogue with the nurse.

" You are not strong enough to talk about it now, nor even to hear me talk much. I shall announce our engagement as soon as I leave here ; and as soon as you are able, we will be married."

The poor man shook his head, and put his hand over his eyes. Eileen kissed the hand. " That 's all now, darling. I only wish you were poor and not rich. Will you lie here, and think of my happiness and yours until I come again ? I must not tire you ; I shall come again to-morrow. I am yours, and you are mine." And slipping a ring off her finger, Eileen placed it upon Mr. Warwick's emaciated hand. "Come, Philippa ! " And she burst from the room before the bewildered man could find breath wherewith to utter a word. Even then he could not call her back, although he tried. He looked at the ring in bewilderment ; he imprinted a timid little kiss upon it ; and sinking back upon his pillow and closing his eyes, he lay dreaming, half unconscious, of the most blissful moment of his life.

" Oh, Eileen," said Philippa, her face blazing, as

they entered the carriage again, to go home (the whole thing had taken hardly five minutes), "what have I been a party to?"

"To the one transaction of my career of which I am not ashamed," returned Eileen, looking heroic, although she seemed on the point of breaking down. "It is odd to you; but you don't know how the dear thing has worshipped me, and how I have driven him about until he has been nearly demented, and he so sweet and gentle and kind through everything! Philippa, love is a word I shall never take upon my lips; but every other noble feeling inspires me when I think of that man."

"And yet without love all the other feelings are nothing," sighed Philippa. "How I wish you were not such a whirlwind, Eileen! And how I wish I knew whether I have done an absolute wrong in letting this thing go on or not."

"You couldn't have stopped it," said Eileen; "so don't disturb yourself on that score."

"I am afraid of you, Eileen," resumed Philippa, "you make my brain reel; and yet I believe I am more in sympathy with this move — if it could only have been made sooner and not so theatrically — than with any of the others. However, let us keep this strictly private at present."

"Private!" cried Eileen; "I shall make my engagement to Mr. Warwick public in another hour."

"I forbid it," said Philippa. "If you have any regard for me, you will not do this and displease me. Mr. Warwick is too ill now; he may not live, Eileen. Wait a few weeks, at least."

"Not a moment!" said Eileen, firmly; and her chin was set beyond appeal; "I can't. I hurried about this because I cannot be rid of Colonel Beverley without something positive to tell him. You don't know him, Philippa; he would never let me go. He is the only man I am afraid of. I am afraid of him when I am alone with him."

"I will stay in the room with you, dear, if you wish it," urged Philippa. "You have a right to change your mind, and he is not coward enough to intimidate you. He is a gentleman."

"Yes, he is; no, he is n't," answered Eileen, to the last two statements. "He had a gleam in his eye, and he means to alarm me into submission. I know him. I shall tell him that I am engaged. He won't tell anybody, you may be sure, and we won't tell any one else for the present, if that will please you, Philippa. But I will see him alone, I would rather; he will never be contented until he does see me, and it 's much better to have it over."

Philippa had to content herself with this compromise.

Eileen, the bold, the daring, felt herself very small and weak when twelve o'clock came, and with it her outraged lover. But she went to meet him, as he came in, with a front of steel. "Colonel Beverley," she said, looking up at him unflinchingly, although a tell-tale trip-hammer in her breast was sending the blood irregularly into her face and out, "I have a piece of news for you."

It was what he had feared then; Jack had lied to him again. He had said he was going off in the

morning; and when Colonel Beverley, in his desperation, trying every means to circumvent him, had
gone to Government House, one of Carbury's servants told him — as a blind, of course, — that the
Captain Sahib (Jack) was ill upstairs. So much for
true morality!

"A piece of news?" he repeated, with kindly surprise; "well, let me hear it. Let's sit down, dearest!
Is your Arab dead? or has Barney eaten one of
his quail? It's sad news, I judge, from your
expression."

"No, not altogether sad," said Eileen, forcing a
smile. "I am engaged to Mr. Warwick, and he,
you know, is frightfully ill. That is the sad part
of it."

Colonel Beverley fastened a piercing look upon
his promised bride of the day before, as well he
might. Eileen was frightened, but she had nerved
herself up to go through any kind of scene, and did
not show her fright.

"Is there insanity in your family?" he asked
with pretended anxiety; and indeed a stronger
man might have been staggered by the rapidity of
Eileen's changes of base.

"Don't speak to me like that!" said Eileen, losing
her temper and stamping her foot angrily. She saw
her mistake now, in not having either refused this
interview altogether, or placed herself on the right
footing, which was disgust at Colonel Beverley's conduct, and a determination to have nothing more to
do with him. Her fear of dragging Jack into a
quarrel with his father had caused her to appear

undignified, erratic, and in fact almost insane. " I
do owe you an explanation, I am aware," she said
more quietly, " and I will give it you."

" Well, considering the fact that I left you late
yesterday only my affianced wife, that 's all, I may
not deserve any explanation of this sudden over-
turning of the whole system of the spheres ; you
know best about that. Don't trouble to tell me
about it, if it 's a bore. Besides, at this rate of
speed, you may be promising yourself to another
man by night ; so why bother about so many explanations? One at the end — if there comes an
end — will do for all."

Eileen stood before the Colonel, a picture of un-
appeasable wrath. " I am accountable to no one
for my actions," she said. " I have changed my
views concerning you, and I would not on any
account marry you, that is all."

" Then you are not engaged to Mr. Warwick? "
Colonel Beverley asked. " Pardon me if I do not
understand, quite. You have engaged yourself to
him since last night, — and he very ill in bed?
Your story has an air of unreality about it. It
seems incredible, in fact."

" I am going to marry Mr. Warwick," she said
boldly, with a large lump in her throat nevertheless.

Colonel Beverley had really grasped the situation
perfectly. He knew that Eileen in a fit of pique
at having been deceived, and really not daring to
change so rapidly from father to son, had thrown
herself, perhaps by letter, into Mr. Warwick's arms.
" Daring little scatter-brain ! " he thought. " Fool-

ish baby! A dead man my rival, eh?" And then
there occurred the pleasing thought, to his machi-
nating mind, that Eileen would be a more suitable
match a year hence, as inheritress of the Warwick
millions. Still, that was only passing; he could not
let slight and humiliation go by so easily.

"Eileen," he said very softly, changing his tone,
"you are only a child, and you have had so much
worry lately that it has unstrung you. You are
mine, you know; I have not released you from our
engagement. It is my duty to look after you.
Now think no more about marriage at present.
Let us be quietly happy. Warwick is very sick;
and much credit as your sweet, sacrificing spirit does
you, you cannot be allowed to go on with that step.
Jack has tried to injure his own father, who, old as
he is in the ways of the world, has no weapon
with which to reply to his stabs in the back. Let
us be patient and wait. Time will right me; I only
ask for that."

"Jack has not tried to injure you," answered
Eileen, loftily. "It is you who tried to injure him,
and succeeded. My peculiar lot forces me into
strange complications, and sometimes I have to
act with lightning-quickness. I cannot argue with
you. I would not listen to you again, if you followed me to the ends of the earth. I shall marry
Mr. Warwick, or remain unmarried."

"And where is Jack?" asked the Colonel, whose
gentleness was fitful. "You have been engaged to
him, I suppose, and thrown him over within the last
twenty-four hours?"

Eileen curled her lip, and started toward the door, without a word. Colonel Beverley caught her by the wrist, and forced her to sit beside him on the sofa. He drew her close to him, and kissed her angry face wildly with fiery kisses. " Eileen," he begged, " don't send me away, — don't, in Heaven's name! What have I done but love you too well? What proof can I give, do you ask? My son is estranged from me on your account; and now you leave me. No, no, darling," for Eileen was making a mad struggle to get away, "you cannot go. You must stay. Let me tell you, dear, I have never begun to tell you the extent of my burning love for you."

Eileen had ceased to struggle; she lay passively against his shoulder, her eyes shut, her muscles relaxed. Colonel Beverley looked anxiously at the quiet figure. He laid her upon the sofa, and seeing her still rigid, ran to ask for water, for fear of alarming the house if he called.

As soon as he was at the end of the room, Eileen opened her eyes, started to her feet, and was out in a fraction of a second. By the time the Colonel returned to the empty sofa, she was in her dressing-room sponging her face vigorously, trying to remove the insulting stains of the kisses which had put the crowning touches to the loathing she should always feel for Colonel Beverley.

CHAPTER XXIV.

"YOU may hear strange 'gup' about me," said Colonel Beverley, laughingly, at the Club, to Tom Carbury, whom he had asked to lunch with him. Colonel Beverley was looking very well; bright and easy, and as young as Jack. "A good deal younger than Jack," thought Carbury, who knew how the poor boy was tossing and turning on his bed at that moment.

"I don't take much stock in 'gup,'" answered Tom, carelessly. He was in rather an uncomfortable position, as regarded Jack, and was lunching with the Colonel partly that he might learn better what to do. There was a wound on Jack's head, which had not been noticed at first; but it had bled and bled, quietly, and had bidden fair to be ugly at one time, owing to delay. It would be a satisfaction to know something.

"I'll tell you the truth, Carbury," the Colonel went on; "it's better you should know. You are a friend of us all, and have been in it somewhat."

Tom looked up. "I'm Jack's friend, you know, Bev," he said distinctly; "you understand that. Nobody says a word against the boy to me. Now go on, if you like."

"Oh, who is n't his friend?" laughed Colonel Beverley, gayly. "Rustic simplicity always fetches the populace. No. Jack, as you know, as everybody knows, was wild — gone — mad over Lady Ellen. I did n't know it for a long time; at least, I did n't choose to know it, because I thought it would die out. I was getting rather deep in that direction myself. I offered to withdraw in Jack's favor, — ridiculous situation, was n't it? — but Jack, who is a filial dog, — if I do say it, who should n't, — offered to withdraw in mine, and did withdraw, by Jove! The very idea of a father and son competing for the same matrimonial prize was distasteful to us both, naturally. In vain I assured Jack that I was not hit; the thought was enough for him. He 's an odd, sentimental dog; and my lady, in a fit of pique at what she calls the desertion of both, is going to marry old Warwick, with both feet in the grave, I hear."

Carbury was not anxious the Colonel should take him for a gullible fool. But he had sworn to Jack. "You are lucky," he said, "in having a son like that; they don't grow on every bush, and I don't know one like him. He 's too honorable; that 's the trouble."

"I 'm not worrying over that," said the Colonel. "His honor won't keep him awake nights. He 's too confoundedly romantic; that 's the trouble. He quarrelled with me for nothing, and won't make up. I don't even know where he is now, do you?"

"Yes," said Carbury, "I know. Old Warwick, they say, can't pull through. Does the girl prefer a corpse to two fine figures of men, like you and Jack?"

"It was not a question of preference," answered the Colonel, mysteriously. "But," he added with a sigh, "I am awfully fond of that charming creature, and life seems dark without her, and really — " And Colonel Beverley tried to pull a long face, and look sad, with a twinkle in his eye.

Carbury kept his counsel, but he remembered too distinctly Jack's bitterness to believe this tale. A simple withdrawal would have raised Jack's esteem for his father, not laid it in the dirt. But he told Jack nothing of all this. And when Jack was able, and just before he left Calcutta, he wrote Eileen a note; and this is what he said : —

"I understand. It is better. The shadow is on our hearts, and you could not have been happy. When we are both old, we can see each other, and my pain may perhaps be dulled, although I do not see any chance of it now. I hope you are not suffering one millionth of this."

And Eileen, who had been through everything lately, with her head high, and who seemed able to bear things which laid strong men low, — Eileen, who had hardly given way once, burst into wild sobs over the little letter.

"Happiness," she said, "what is it? There is never any for me. And since Jack has known me, he has had little. And that other, that dear one to whom I belong now, — he is just beginning to know it now that he can have almost none."

There was a short, a very short period of happiness for Mr. Warwick. He rallied temporarily under Eileen's ministrations, and at one time they thought he might be got on board ship to go home. But he failed again steadily. It was too late to save his life.

But Eileen retrieved a part of the trouble she had made him, and indeed she exaggerated her own fault in the matter.

And then he died, — brave, patient, happy Mr. Warwick ! He had had three weeks of bliss unspeakable, with Eileen reading to him, talking gently to him, or when he grew too weak for reading or talking, sitting with her hand in his, giving him his draughts, and letting him see her complete serenity in his presence. He had worried a little over one thing. He did not like to think that she had come simply out of pity, and to nurse him ; and he could not bear to think of her young life ruined for the second time. " Dearest," he said once feebly, " did you care for either of the Beverleys ? "

" For Jack, dear," she said softly ; " but I was engaged to his father — for about a minute," she added archly.

" For Jack," he repeated a long time after ; " can you not marry him by and by ? "

She shook her head. " No, darling."

" I wish you could," he said wearily. " I could die so much more easily if I thought you would be happily married."

" I am happy now," she said, " or I should be if you were well. If you will get strong, and leave the horrid money to somebody else, I shall be the happiest woman in the world."

That night he died. And when Eileen came in the morning to sit with him, they told her. She had learned to live for him; he filled all her thoughts, and she mourned him very sorely.

CHAPTER XXV.

TWO years after Mr. Warwick's death, the Winterfords and Eileen were living in London, where they had been for a year. Barney had some kind of an appointment in the India office, and was enjoying London life like a school-boy, — happy and gay with his children, not in the least fatherly, but knowing enough not to set a bad example to his boys. Altogether the Winterford star was high in the firmament.

Eileen had had the Warwick millions forced upon her, after all. There were no relatives to contest the will, as she had at first hoped. The will had been made while Eileen was on her way to Ceylon with the Maynards.

Eileen could not change her nature, and she was still gay in her manner. But the gayness was subdued, and she had lost her wildness in a great measure. The money had brought heavy responsibilities, and she had insisted upon devoting half her income to her nephews and nieces. This eased the whole household in Eccleston Square, for Philippa would always live with her father, and gave Eileen a happy feeling of usefulness.

Colonel Beverley had been intimate at their Calcutta house up to the last minute. He wore a distant, yet reverential air, to which Eileen outwardly paid no attention, but which she saw, of course. He spoke most feelingly of Mr. Warwick, and extended deep sympathy in little ways to Eileen, who refused to receive it. But after they sailed they had heard only occasionally from him.

Mrs. Maynard was stopping with Eileen at her house in Mayfair; and one day when Eileen and Philippa were driving home, expecting to find her there, they came upon two familiar figures turning a corner. "Why," exclaimed Philippa, without noticing a very crimson change which had bespread Eileen's cheek, "if there are not Captain Carbury and Jack Beverley! How delightful!" And leaning from the window she bowed to the two men, who instantly came to the carriage.

"Well, if here is not a bit of India!" cried Carbury; "the largest half, rather. Do let us both come and see you this very day! We're lost in London, where nobody remembers us, or cares about us, if they do."

Philippa gave them her number, and begged them to come at once.

"And are you living with Barney?" asked Captain Beverley, in a low voice, of Eileen. He had hardly spoken before. He had been doing some great work in the Transvaal and the Soudan, and had had decorations without number.

"Oh, no," Philippa laughed, "Eileen's a grand lady now, with a house of her own right here."

"And may I come there?"

Eileen bowed. They were both awkward.

After the men had gone, Philippa took Eileen's hand in hers. "Don't be silly any longer, Eileen! Jack Beverley is evidently as much in love as ever; he deserves something from you. You let him get where he is now. I heard he was in London, and I hope he has come to some purpose. You have acted hitherto on your own impulses, Eileen, and they have brought you into great unhappiness. Be ruled by me now, dear!"

"Two years is a long time," remarked Eileen, quietly. "I have no reason to think Captain Beverley unchanged." But although her tone was quiet, she had very hard work to keep herself so. The sight of Jack had brought back everything, — harrowing scenes, exciting crises, wild actions, miserable moments. She had not grown pale and pined, as most women do under unhappiness. Something — her hard heart, she said — had almost always kept her from giving way or being ill. It often mortified her to think how much she could stand. Now, to Philippa's surprise, she seemed thoroughly unnerved. She trembled, and for once she did not go on with the talk. When they had reached home, she threw herself on a couch, and sobbed until Philippa grew alarmed. When the fit subsided, "I am afraid of life," Eileen sobbed; "I am afraid to live on. There is always some question to decide, and I always decide wrong. I am forever doing theatrical, extravagant things, you tell me. I can't help it. I blush, Philippa, when I

think how frantic I must have driven you by my
extremes when we were in Calcutta; and yet I am
so little changed that if I had it all to do over
again, I could do no differently, — that is, if matters
came to such crises."

"You *make* matters difficult, Eileen," said Philippa, " by seeing them in out-of-the-way lights, and
by taking things into your own hands. Of course
I don't know now about Jack Beverley; but if he
asks you to marry him, and you love him, why, do
so, that 's all."

" I can't make a quarrel in a family," said Eileen.
"If I go into this one, I do that. If I stay
out, I do not make Jack any more miserable than
he has been all this time, — nor myself either, I
suppose."

" There you are," said Philippa; " that 's what I
mean. *You* have to decide this momentous question of the quarrel between father and son, when
you have nothing to do with it. Let them settle it
between themselves. You need not marry Jack's
father; and as there is no longer a family house
where you are all obliged to meet, there will be no
disagreeable encounters."

" Oh, dear," said Eileen, burying her face in the
pillow again, " I don't see why I can't have a little bit
of happiness. I never have had any, — not real, personal happiness of my own, I mean. Lately I have
had reflected and impersonal happiness, but I am
selfish enough to want some of the other kind. I
never have been happy," she went on, in a pathetically childish way, "except that little time in Cal-

cutta when Jack was with me ; and then I was n't
really," she added, half laughing, "because I did n't
know enough to be."

Mrs. Maynard, who had worried over Eileen not
a little, arrived later in the day, and found her
quite recovered from her outburst of the morning,
bright and apparently happy. "I must talk about
that dear man," Mrs. Maynard said. (Eileen had
written her often, and she knew what had happened.) "It was a blessed thing you went to him,
dear girl."

"I did the thing in my usual way," said Eileen,
sadly, — "helter-skelter, thunder and lightning ; but
I am thankful I went. He was ecstatic ; and I had
a glow about my heart I shall never cease to feel.
I only regret we could not have been married. I
wanted the right to mourn him and to bear his
name." Eileen always spoke in this calm way of
Mr. Warwick.

"It was better as it came about," said Mrs. Maynard, gently. "I was proud of you, dear, and I know
he enjoyed more in those few weeks of your presence than he had suffered in his life. A great, noble
heart he had ; and curiously enough, such a sensitive
organization that he could not help giving way
under your rejection."

"Do you think it killed him?" asked Eileen, in
a horrified tone, with great round eyes.

"No, no," said Mrs. Maynard ; "he was under a
doctor's care for something, — an Indian liver, I believe, — when we first knew him, Mr. Maynard
says. He could not have lived many years."

" Jack Beverley is in London," said Eileen, shyly.
" Did you see him at Calcutta? "

" I never met either of the Beverley men," answered Mrs. Maynard. " I have heard so much about them, however. A Calcutta woman told me that both were devoted to you, — the father particularly."

" He was devoted to untruth," said Eileen, " and me incidentally. I disliked him extremely at last. Jack is quite different, and one of my best friends." So Eileen admitted the Captain to her friendship ; that was one point scored for him.

Philippa came in for a cup of tea, and to see Mrs. Maynard, at five. " I left word for our two Calcutta men to come here," she said. " They had not appeared when I left." And the words were hardly out of her mouth before the two appeared.

Captain Carbury asked them all to go to the theatre that night. " And to dine at the Criterion too," he said. " Will you ask Barney? That is, if you will dine in a restaurant, Lady Barney, and you other grand ladies? "

" We were to dine here," Philippa said. " Eileen can't waste a whole dinner ; so I invite you in her name to come here too ! "

So it was settled ; and there was a merry, reunited lot that night dining together. Jack had the post farthest from that of honor ; he sat where he could see Eileen, however. She was in white and gold, and looked like a piece of rare porcelain, he thought. Her voice was like the music of the spheres to him, and her face was a poem and a picture combined. He should not tell her of his love, nor approach her. But to be in the party was unsafe, and Jack resolved he could not come so near the fire again.

All Eileen's old frank manner with him was gone; she addressed him rather timidly, and her hand was cold when he took it. Eileen's impulse might be to throw herself into Mr. Warwick's arms; she was as shy as a school-girl with this boyish lover. Jack's boyishness, however, had nearly departed; he was really perceptibly gray, and his face was worn, for so young a man.

" Now," said Barney, gayly, " here 's to our very jolly reunion, and to these good visitors of ours, and to you Jacky and Tommy, returned Anglos ! I 'm as good as I was, barrin' a foot, and the rest of you look better than never; and all we want now is old Bev, to complete the party."

Barney knew little of the revolutions in the family. He had seen Colonel Beverley's devotion, but supposed that it had died out somehow, and was glad of it.

" Where is your father? " asked Philippa, gently.

" In England," answered Jack; " he has been here for a few weeks, and is coming to London to-morrow."

Eileen did not change her countenance in the least. Jack's was the only name which had ever had the power to make her show outward agitation.

In the carriage, at the theatre, the two were still separated, although Philippa tried to arrange their seats together. Eileen deliberately turned her chair so that no one could speak confidentially to her, and Jack had no idea of trying to do so. She knew he loved her; he knew she loved him; neither would ever dare give the first sign. His father's treachery had humiliated Jack; his own hand seemed soiled now.

"I have not had *my* dinner yet," said Tom Carbury, as he was putting on Eileen's wrap. "My leave is so short, and I hate so going back to that wretched India, that I am going to make the most of you dear people. Shall we say Friday? And where shall the dinner be?"

"Oh, don't throw away your money, Tom!" said Barney. "Come and dine with *us* on Friday. Our cook has the touch of a Meisonnier, and his dinners are as finished."

"They taste of oil too," said Eileen. "He has a decidedly Italian bent."

"Not at all," argued Barney. "Frenchmen use oil too; you're not half trained if you don't know the proper use of olive oil." And Barney went on explaining his theories, as they left the box.

"Another evening with Jack," thought Eileen. "Another evening with Eileen," thought Jack. Not two words had they exchanged, nor one glance; but whole discourses and all the eyesight in the world would not have meant more than their constrained silences. They both felt, every instant; and all through the play, Eileen knew that Jack was thinking only of her. Jack himself was not so sure of Eileen.

Mrs. Maynard was not deceived long. She saw in a few hours that Eileen was still unsettled, still ill at ease. " There is no use in prescribing employment for her," she said to herself. "To marry is her vocation."

Eileen would not speak of Jack again. She thought about nothing but the Friday night when she was to see him again, estranged, awkward, to be sure, but still breathing the same air. How little she knew of his past now ! How she longed to ask him about it ! She did not dare open the floodgates, however ; for there would be no stop then, she knew.

One night coming home from a dinner, she saw him walking near her house. " Patient boy ! " she said to herself. And yet she did not know whether it was the patience of hopeless resignation or of stifled hope. Jack did not know which it was, either.

Jack was dreading the sight of his father. He had not seen him at all, and he hoped he should not. On the Thursday, Barney and Jack were at their Club together, when Colonel Beverley came in.

" Well, Paddy," he exclaimed joyously, at sight of them, " I was just thinking of looking you up ; and you, my dear boy," he said, shaking Jack warmly by the rather limp hand, " come to me ; I 've a lodging for you next mine."

" I 'm very comfortable, sir, thank you, with Carbury," answered Jack, quietly. He was amazed to find his father looking so young and well. He himself had had no good looks to lose, but he knew he was looking poorly. It was a strange feeling the sight of the man who had once been everything to him awakened. He was ashamed of him now, and once he had been so proud!

"Come to-morrow and dine," said Barney. "We've an Indian party, and some Americans — awfully good sort — stopping with Eileen. Do come!"

Jack said not a word; but he felt an indisposition coming on which would prevent his attendance on the following night.

"Will you dine with me here to-night, Jack?" asked Colonel Beverley, kindly.

Barney had turned away to speak to a group of men.

"No," said Jack, curtly, "I'll not dine with you, sir."

"Now look here, Jack," said the Colonel, taking him by the arm, to Jack's disgust, and leading him into a window-recess from which they could be seen on the street, looking very familiar and happy together. "It's our misfortune to have had bitter words. But I am your father, and I have a right to demand civil treatment from you, at least in public. That's all I ask; do you hear me?"

Jack bowed. "I hear you, sir; you shall have civil treatment from me — in public." And he turned to walk away.

"Nonsense, boy! you know what I mean," said the Colonel, testily. "You must come and stay in the same lodgings, or people will talk."

"I will leave London at once, sir, this very night,"

Jack replied, "rather than do that; and in fact I have decided to do so, at any rate." And he turned quickly back to a knot of men, to avoid further argument.

Colonel Beverley grated his teeth together, and ground his heel into the floor. "I should n't mind quarrelling with the fool nor killing him, but everybody knows what the quarrel is about. Well, I shall take the bull by the horns, and walk straight into the enemy's camp now." And he hailed a hansom outside, having learned Eileen's number from Barney, and drove to her house.

Jack, when he left the Club, had walked aimlessly, and yet in the direction of Park Lane, unconscious of it as he thought himself to be. To leave London, and not to see her again; to be thrust out of Paradise for the second time when he was contented with just looking at her, — oh, how cruel his fate! He must explain to Eileen and to Philippa his proposed defection. One visit would have done for both; but he went, it is needless to say, to Eileen's house first.

Mrs. Maynard and Eileen were in the morning-room, and *his father* was with them! Impotent rage and despair seized poor Jack. It was too late to draw back, so he went boldly forward. "Thank Heaven for Mrs. Maynard's restraining presence!" both Jack and Eileen fervently ejaculated to themselves. The visit was cold and formal. Eileen had never meant to see Colonel Beverley, but it could not be helped.

After a few minutes Jack rose stiffly, and said,

"I am going to see Lady Barney now, to make my excuses for to-morrow night."

"Excuses? What a pity to spoil our cosey party!" said Mrs. Maynard.

"I want to show you a painting of my niece Biddy Winterford," said Eileen, desperately. "Will you come to the drawing-room?"

"May I not see it too?" asked Colonel Beverley. But Eileen, although he spoke distinctly, pretended not to hear, and he could not leave Mrs. Maynard alone. So Jack and Eileen were together.

They went into the drawing-room, and Jack looked at the portrait of Biddy, although he did not see a feature nor a stroke of it. "I am going away, Eileen," he said, "to-night. It is of no use; I cannot bear it. I am a coward; not to be with you always is the awful thought which is coming before me every moment, and I must run away from it."

Eileen did not know how she came to lure Jack off in this fashion. It was the straw at which the drowning man clutches, she thinks now. She could not see him leave her forever without a word. This sight of him had roused the old feeling, strengthened it, and added a hundred new feelings. She must at least say good-by to him alone!

She stammered out a criticism of the portrait. "It wants something," she said; "I don't know exactly what it wants."

"I know exactly what *I* want," said Jack. "And if I can't have it, the next thing I pray for is numbness, — the capacity not to suffer. Oh, Eileen, your

little note, when you told me you *did* care, put
new strength into me, — but only to love you more
with. It all goes to that. In other respects I am
as weak as a baby."

"So am I," said Eileen. And then she turned
her head away, and Jack could not help seizing her
hand. "I loved you when you were poor, Eileen,"
he said softly. "I wish you were so now. But if we
love each other — and we do?" — Eileen looked up
into his face with a gaze which settled that point
beyond a question, — "why should anything come
between us, after all?"

"Something has come between us," answered
Eileen, sadly; "but I sometimes have thought we
both of us exaggerated the shadow a little, — now
that I am older and have learned wisdom."

"Oh," said Jack, with almost a groan, "you precious thing!"

This was not a logical answer, but they were beyond logic. To repeat what they said now would be
taking an unfair advantage of both. Jack looked
down upon the golden hair, the sweet face down-
turned, the little hands folded in her lap. He whispered softly to her, and Eileen's face looked at him
then full of radiance, and in her eyes were tears.
The happy fate of the strong, steadfast man and the
wilful, capricious woman was settled.

Colonel Beverley prolonged his visit far beyond
the customary limit, and at last, with a farewell for
his impolite hostess, went gayly (and angrily) away.
Mrs. Maynard sat smiling softly to herself as the
hours went, and the two wanderers did not return.

She was just going to dress for dinner, when she saw their shadows in the doorway.

They thought she had gone. Eileen's face was luminous; her eyes were gleaming softly, her lips quivering with joy. Mrs. Maynard slipped out by a side door. "This is her rightful lover," she said. "No one has ever called that look into her face before. How thankful I am she is happy and at rest!"

THE END.

UPTON'S HANDBOOKS ON MUSIC.

Comprising The Standard Operas, The Standard Oratorios, The Standard Cantatas, The Standard Symphonies.

By GEORGE P. UPTON. 12mo, flexible cloth, extra, per volume, $1.50; extra gilt, gilt edges, $2.00.

The same in neat box, per set, cloth $6.00
,,   ,,   ,,   ,,   extra gilt 8.00
,,   ,,   ,,   ,,   half calf, gilt tops . 13.00
,,   ,,   ,,   ,,   half moro., gilt tops 14.00
,,   ,,   ,,   ,,   half moro., gilt edges 15.00
,,   ,,   ,,   ,,   tree calf, gilt edges 22.00

Of the Standard Operas, R. H. Stoddard, in "Evening Mail and Express" (New York) says:

"Among the multitude of handbooks described by easy-going writers of book-notices as supplying a long-felt want, we know of none which so completely carries out the intention of the writer as 'The Standard Operas,' by Mr. George P. Upton, whose object is to present to his readers a comprehensive sketch of each of the operas contained in the modern repertory. . . . There are thousands of music-loving people who will be glad to have the kind of knowledge which Mr. Upton has collected for their benefit, and has cast in a clear and compact form."

Of the Standard Oratorios, the "Nation" (New York) says:

"Music-lovers are under a new obligation to Mr. Upton for this companion to his "Standard Operas," — two books which deserve to be placed on the same shelf with Grove's and Riemann's musical dictionaries."

Of the Standard Cantatas, the "Boston Post" says:

"Mr. Upton has done a genuine service to the cause of music and to all music-lovers in the preparation of this work, and that service is none the less important in that while wholly unassuming and untechnical, it is comprehensive, scholarly, and thorough."

Of the Standard Symphonies, the "Home Journal" (New York) says:

"None who have seen the previous books of Mr. Upton will need assurance that this is as indispensable as the others to one who would listen intelligently to that better class of music which musicians congratulate themselves Americans are learning to appreciatively enjoy."

Sold by all booksellers, or mailed, post-paid, on receipt of price, by

A. C. McCLURG & CO., PUBLISHERS,

COR. WABASH AVE. AND MADISON ST., CHICAGO.

TALES FROM FOREIGN TONGUES.

MEMORIES. A Story of German Love. By
MAX MULLER.

GRAZIELLA. A Story of Italian Love. By
ALPHONSE DE LAMARTINE.

MADELEINE. A Story of French Love. By
JULES SANDEAU.

M A R I E. A Story of Russian Love. By
ALEXANDER PUSHKIN.

In cloth, gilt top, per volume. $1.00
The same, in neat box, per set 4.00
In half calf or morocco, gilt top, per set 9.00
In half calf or morocco, gilt edges, per set . . . 10.00
In flexible calf or russia, gilt edges, per set . . 12.00

The series of four volumes forms, perhaps, the choicest
addition to the literature of the English language that has
been made in recent years.

Of "Memories," the London *Academy* says: "It is a prose
poem. . . . Its beauty and pathos show us a fresh phase of a
many-sided mind, to which we already owe large debts of
gratitude."

Of "Graziella," the Boston *Post* says: "It is full of beautiful sentiment, unique and graceful in style, of course, as were
all the writings of this distinguished French author."

Of "Madeleine," the New York *Evening Mail* says: "It is
one of the most exquisite love tales that ever was written,
abounding in genuine pathos and sparkling wit, and so pure in
its sentiment that it may be read by a child."

Of "Marie," the Cincinnati *Gazette* says: "It is one of the
purest, sweetest little narratives that we have read for a long
time. It is a little classic, and a Russian classic, too."

Sold by all booksellers, or mailed on receipt of price, by
A. C. McCLURG & CO., PUBLISHERS,
COR. WABASH AVE. AND MADISON ST., CHICAGO.

SESAME AND LILIES.

THREE LECTURES BY JOHN RUSKIN.

I. OF KINGS' TREASURES.
II. OF QUEENS' GARDENS.
III. OF THE MYSTERY OF LIFE.

12mo, 201 pages, gilt top.   Price, $1.00.

In half calf or half morocco, gilt top, $2.75.
In limp russia or limp morocco, gilt edges, $3.50.

———

One of the most popular as well as most valuable of Ruskin's works is "Sesame and Lilies," and this has been brought out by McClurg & Co. in a neat and handy volume of good print and excellent paper. The publishers have wisely inserted in this volume Ruskin's admirable and thoroughly characteristic preface which he prepared for the new and revised edition of his works in 1871. The size, shape, and compactness of this issue make it an admirable pocket companion for desultory reading in the cars, in the woods, or at the shore. — *Evening Transcript, Boston.*

Other editions of this notable and popular book have been printed, but none so tastefully as this. Of the book itself it may not be inopportune to say that it shows the author at his best, being devoted to life instead of art, and embodying Ruskin's earnestness and gift of language without calling attention to any of his oddities and hobbies. — *Herald, New York.*

It would be hard to find a better book to put into the hands of a youth — boy or girl — at that epoch of life when the spiritual and intellectual faculties seem to leap out with a bound from the chrysalis of the animal nature and determine their direction for life. — *Home Journal, New York.*

The book is one by all means to be commended to young women and young men who care for refinement of character and purity of heart and earnestness of purpose, and who are able to appreciate noble thought clothed in exquisite diction. — *Evangelist, New York.*

———

Sold by all booksellers, or mailed, on receipt of price, by

A. C. McCLURG & CO., PUBLISHERS,
COR. WABASH AVE. AND MADISON ST., CHICAGO.

THE AZTECS. Their History, Manners, and Customs. From the French of LUCIEN BIART. Authorized translation by J. L. GARNER.

Illustrated, 8vo, 340 pages, price, $2.00.

The author has travelled through the country of whose former glories his book is a recital, and his studies and discoveries leaven the book throughout. The volume is absorbingly interesting, and is as attractive in style as it is in material. — *Saturday Evening Gazette, Boston.*

Nowhere has this subject been more fully and intelligently treated than in this volume, now placed within reach of American readers. The mythology of the Aztecs receives special attention, and all that is known of their lives, their hopes, their fears, and aspirations finds record here. — *The Tribune, Chicago.*

The man who can rise from the study of Lucien Biart's invaluable work, "The Aztecs," without feelings of amazement and admiration for the history and the government, and for the arts cultivated by these Romans of the New World is not to be envied. — *The Advance, Chicago.*

The twilight origin of the present race is graphically presented; those strange people whose traces have almost vanished from off the face of the earth again live before us. Their taxes and tributes, their marriage ceremonies, their burial customs, laws, medicines, food, poetry, and dances are described . . . The book is a very interesting one, and is brought out with copious illustrations. — *The Traveller, Boston.*

M. Biart is the most competent authority living on the subject of the Aztecs. He spent many years in Mexico, studied his subject carefully through all means of information, and wrote his book from the view-point of a scientist. His style is very attractive, and it has been very successfully translated. The general reader, as well as all scholars, will be much taken with the work. — *Chronicle Telegraph, Pittsburg.*

Sold by all booksellers, or mailed on receipt of price, by

A. C. McCLURG & CO., PUBLISHERS,

COR. WABASH AVE. AND MADISON ST., CHICAGO.

THE STORY OF TONTY.

AN HISTORICAL ROMANCE.

By Mrs. MARY HARTWELL CATHERWOOD.

12mo, 224 pages. Price, $1.25.

"The Story of Tonty" is eminently a Western story, beginning at Montreal, tarrying at Fort Frontenac, and ending at the old fort at Starved Rock, on the Illinois River. It weaves the adventures of the two great explorers, the intrepid La Salle and his faithful lieutenant, Tonty, into a tale as thrilling and romantic as the descriptive portions are brilliant and vivid. It is superbly illustrated with twenty-three masterly drawings by Mr. Enoch Ward.

Such tales as this render service past expression to the cause of history. They weave a spell in which old chronicles are vivified and breathe out human life Mrs. Catherwood, in thus bringing out from the treasure-houses of half-forgotten historical record things new and old, has set herself one of the worthiest literary tasks of her generation, and is showing herself finely adequate to its fulfilment. — *Transcript, Boston.*

A powerful story by a writer newly sprung to fame. . . . All the century we have been waiting for the deft hand that could put flesh upon the dry bones of our early heroes. Here is a recreation indeed. . . . One comes from the reading of the romance with a quickened interest in our early national history, and a profound admiration for the art that can so transport us to the dreamful realms where fancy is monarch of fact. — *Press, Philadelphia.*

"The Story of Tonty" is full of the atmosphere of its time. It betrays an intimate and sympathetic knowledge of the great age of explorers, and it is altogether a charming piece of work. — *Christian Union, New York.*

Original in treatment, in subject, and in all the details of *mise en scene*, it must stand unique among recent romances. — *News, Chicago.*

Sold by all booksellers, or mailed, on receipt of price, by

A. C. McCLURG & CO., PUBLISHERS,

COR. WABASH AVE. AND MADISON ST., CHICAGO.

THE HUMBLER POETS. A Collection of Newspaper and Periodical Verse. 1870 to 1885. By SLASON THOMPSON. Crown 8vo, 459 pages, cloth, gilt top. Price, $2.00.

In half calf or half morocco, $4.00.

————◆————

The publishers have done well in issuing this volume in a style of literary and artistic excellence, such as is given to the works of the poets of name and fame, because the contents richly entitle it to such distinction. — *Home Journal, Boston.*

The high poetic character of these poems, as a whole, is surprising. As a unit, the collection makes an impression which even a genius of the highest order would not be adequate to produce. . . . Measured by poetic richness, variety, and merit of the selections contained, the collection is a rarely good one flavored with the freshness and aroma of the present time. — *Independent, New York.*

Mr. Thompson winnowed out the chaff from the heap, and has given us the golden grain in this volume. Many old newspaper favorites will be recognized in this collection, — many of those song-waifs which have been drifting up and down the newspaper world for years, and which nobody owns but everybody loves. We are glad for ourselves that some one has been kind and tender-hearted enough to take in these fugitive children of the Muses and give them a safe and permanent home. The selection has been made with rare taste and discrimination, and the result is a delightful volume. — *Observer, New York.*

————◆————

Sold by all booksellers, or mailed on receipt of price, by

A. C. McCLURG & CO., PUBLISHERS,

COR. WABASH AVE. AND MADISON ST., CHICAGO.

www.ingramcontent.com/pod-product-compliance
Lightning Source LLC
Chambersburg PA
CBHW030352270326
41926CB00009B/1065